HIDDEN
HISTORY
of
PLANO

HIDDEN
HISTORY
of
PLANO

Mary Jacobs, Jeff Campbell and Cheryl Smith

WITH THE PLANO CONSERVANCY FOR HISTORIC PRESERVATION

THE
History
PRESS

Published by The History Press
Charleston, SC
www.historypress.com

Front cover and back cover, top: Plano Public Library.
Back cover, bottom: Franklin D. Roosevelt Library Public Domain Photographs.

First published 2020

Manufactured in the United States

ISBN 9781467142946

Library of Congress Control Number: 2019954257

Frances Imogene "Gene" Jackson Edwards
March 8, 1939–March 9, 2019

In 2019, we mourned the passing of a great Texan, Gene Edwards. Gene was one of Plano's pioneers of historic preservation and was instrumental in "saving" the George House, which was located on what is now the site of Plano Municipal Center. The George House has been moved to Old City Park in Dallas. Gene was also instrumental in preserving the Texas Electric Railway Plano Station (now the Interurban Railway Museum).

Gene and her husband, Jim, owned the iconic Carpenter "Edwards" House at 1211 16th Street, which was the home of Plano's first mayor, Gip Carpenter, and became a popular wedding venue in the 1990s–2000s. Jim Edwards served as mayor of Plano for two terms from 1978 to 1982.

Gene was also chairman of the Plano Parks Board in the 1980s and was the first chairman of the City of Plano's Historical Commission, now the Heritage Commission.

Gene vowed to celebrate her eightieth birthday on March 8, 2019. When the party was over, she was ecstatic, thankful and very tired. So early that evening, she decided to nap. According to her obituary, "With her head and her heart full of dreams and laughter and love and life, of that day and 80 years before, she drifted asleep. And never woke up. Just as she and God had always planned."

The obituary adds that Gene Edwards "taught us all how to love, how to be faithful, and how to fight; three traits she remained unmatched in, even until the end." May we all remember her example.

CONTENTS

CONTENTS

Acknowledgements

The authors would like to thank:

Renée Burke Jordan, AICP, park planning manager at the City of Plano, for assistance in the story on Plano's oldest tree.

Candace Fountoulakis for researching and writing the chapter on the Collinwood House "mystery" cornerstone.

Jessica Woods of the Plano Conservancy for Historic Preservation, whose careful proofreading of the manuscript saved us from embarrassment.

Jennifer Shertzer for sharing photos for this volume and for her ongoing dedication to telling the story of Plano's rich history in *Plano Magazine*.

Debbie Calvin for her assistance in assembling the "Mayhem on the Interurban" exhibit for the Interurban Railway Museum, the source for "Death on the Rail."

Harold Larson, president of the Board of the Plano Conservancy for Historic Preservation, for his support of this project.

INTRODUCTION

As a young man, William Faulkner had a revelation: "I discovered that my own little postage stamp of native soil was worth writing about and that I would never live long enough to exhaust it."

Faulkner made a conscious effort to treat Oxford, Mississippi, as the seat of his fictional Yoknapatawpha County. I have always found it quite amazing to discover the historic stories and characters in the sphere of where we live and work. The little postage stamp of Plano, Texas, also holds an abundance of historical stories of human triumph and tragedy.

When I first came to work for the Plano Conservancy for Historic Preservation in 2013, I read and researched all of the city's history I could find. One of the first tales I stumbled across was the state championship win of the 1965 Plano Wildcats football team. This was Plano's first state championship—and took place just a year after Plano High School integrated in 1964. A school that integrates one year and wins its first football state championship the next? That sounds like a Disney movie. The story of the 1965 Plano Wildcats football team was chronicled in The History Press book *Football and Integration in Plano, Texas: Stay in There, Wildcats!* It's just one of the fascinating hidden history stories found within the Plano city limits.

We hope you enjoy these stories of Plano's hidden history and that you'll be encouraged to look for the hidden stories in your own little postage stamp of native soil.

—Jeff Campbell
Executive Director, Plano Conservancy for Historic Preservation

A Brief History of Plano

Authors' note: To really appreciate Plano hidden history, you need an overview of the city's history and development. Here's a short version of Plano's past, with a nod to the hidden history with origins in each key period of time.

Early Settlers (1842–72)

Population, 1870: 155

Opportunity brings people to Plano from around the world. It's true today, and it was true in the city's earliest days. For Plano's first settlers, that opportunity came in the form of land.

In 1841, the Republic of Texas was in financial straits, and its "very existence depended on attracting people to settle the vast expanse of land."[1] The republic contracted with twenty men to start the Peters Colony in North Texas in exchange for free land. A married man received 640 acres; a single man got 320 acres. Settlers were expected to live on the land for three years, build a cabin and fence and cultivate at least 15 acres. The area that's now Plano was particularly attractive to farmers because it offered "the best and richest blackland in North Texas and was thought by many to be the best in the United States."[2]

Postcard of Plano, Texas, looking east, around 1902. *Plano Public Library, Plano, Texas.*

Life was hard on the frontier, but a community soon emerged. By 1850, the Plano area had its first school, its first cemetery and a Methodist class, the beginnings of what today is First United Methodist Church of Plano.

Among Plano's earliest settlers was Henry Cook, a man in his seventies who led a caravan of settlers to Texas; his legacy is still evident in Plano today. William Forman I became the first official postmaster, and the name Plano was established. Forman's son built the oldest house still occupied in Plano today, now home to a shop called the Wooden Spoon. Also built around this time was the Collinwood House, another of Plano's oldest existing homes, although its links to Plano's earliest history weren't discovered until 2014.

Another of Plano's first settlers, C.S. Haggard, traveled from Kentucky in a covered wagon, hauling an exceptionally big and strong male donkey named Mammoth Jack. Mammoth Jack went on to sire a line of mules that, by 1866, had earned Plano the moniker of Mule Capital of the World.

The Civil War (1861–65) brought growth to a standstill in Plano. Union sentiments were strong because most settlers had come from the upper South—Kentucky and Tennessee—making Collin County one of the few counties in the state to oppose secession. The settlers owned relatively few enslaved persons, and as a result, "Collin County developed with more of a Midwestern culture than a southern one, which meant that the area had more artisans and professionals."[3]

POSTWAR PROSPERITY (1872–1900)

Population, 1900: 1,304

With the arrival of the railroad linking McKinney and Dallas in 1872, life changed dramatically in Plano. Downtown became the prosperous center of a booming farm economy, thanks to the emergence of cotton as a cash crop, cheap fencing in the form of barbed wire and the development of mechanized farm equipment. The city was incorporated in 1873.

Congregations built churches, and proprietors opened businesses downtown. City leaders established Plano's school system, with the first high school class graduating in 1892. The mayor's office, city council and city court were also established in 1881, meeting the first and third Tuesdays of each month in the back of a saddlery shop. By 1898, Plano even fielded its own Plano Nine Baseball Team, later named the Rough Riders, which emerged as a statewide powerhouse.

During this pivotal period, Plano also faced many challenges. Fires plagued the downtown area, destroying multiple buildings downtown in 1881, 1889, 1895 and again in 1897. City leaders responded by establishing a fire department and building a water system. Many downtown businesses and homes still have wells created during this period. Medical care on the frontier was still relatively limited, and death was a part of daily life, as you'll see in the chapter "Death Is a Salesman."

Four of Olney Davis's five daughters pose in hats, probably in the early twentieth century, when the Gibson Girl look was popular. *Plano Public Library, Plano, Texas.*

SMALL-TOWN PLANO (1900–50)

Population, 1950: 2,126

In the first half of the twentieth century, Plano transitioned from a frontier community into a small but forward-looking town. By the mid-1900s, the annual Old Settlers Reunion Picnic and Barbecue had faded away as the city's original settlers died.

During this time, city leaders led the establishment of a modern infrastructure—electricity and telephone service, trash collection and a sewer system, as well as parcel post, airmail and door-to-door mail service. In 1925, Plano was one of the first towns of its size in Texas with paved streets.

In 1908, the Texas Electric Railway began service that linked Denison and Dallas by way of Plano. That brought commerce to Plano, as well as crime and mayhem. A few years later, a talented young man named L.A. Davis arrived and established himself as a leading African American businessman in Jim Crow Texas. He eventually bought and sold the land that is now the Douglass Community.

Churches were the center of social life and strongly influenced Plano's culture. In 1902, the community resoundingly voted liquor and saloons out of Plano and kept them out for the next eighty years. Blue laws kept businesses shuttered on Sundays.

Postcard of Plano, Texas, looking west, around 1902. Note the interurban depot on the right. *Plano Public Library, Plano, Texas.*

Schools, libraries and civic organizations also flourished during this time. By 1913, Plano High School had organized football and baseball teams; in 1925, the Plano Wildcats celebrated their first undefeated season. The Thursday Study Club, Plano's first literary club, formed in 1914. That group of young ladies later contributed to the World War II effort with a unique recycling project that turned silk hose into backpacks in 1942.

A few years later, fear swept across the nation with the polio epidemic. The Plano Fire Department was prepared, after citizens rallied to purchase Plano's iron lung to help save the lives of children struck by the disease.

As the economy boomed after World War II, cars became more affordable, quickly displacing railways as the main source of transportation and leading to the close of the interurban railway in 1948. Around the same time, the Hunt family began buying farmland to develop in Plano and surrounding areas. By 1950, Plano was on the verge of another period of great change.

Growing Bedroom Community (1950–80)

Population, 1980: 72,330

Plano's years as a farming-based economy came to a close around 1950 with the arrival of small industry and the reappraisal of land values for tax purposes.

Probably the single most important factor contributing to Plano's growth was the extension of North Central Expressway from Campbell Road to Plano in 1957. Plano became a prime destination for people who worked in Dallas but wanted to live in a more suburban environment. By 1960, Plano had become the fastest-growing city in Collin County.

One of those new developments—called Dallas North Estates, because at the time nobody had heard of Plano—boasted a unique amenity, the Texas Pool, shaped like the Lone Star State.

One of the oddest new buildings to pop up in Plano was a pagoda, the centerpiece of Plano University, the brainchild of a man named Robert J. Morris. Some thought he was a visionary; others said he was a con man. He was also responsible for acquiring Plano's first, and only, military tank.

While Plano was expanding, war was escalating in Vietnam. One Plano native distinguished himself with his bravery and sacrifice. The sacrifice of Russell A. Steindam is still remembered today.

Ahead of other cities in North Texas, Plano ISD voluntarily initiated desegregation in the 1964–65 school year at Plano High. Athletics helped unite the Anglo and African American communities, as the Plano High School Wildcats captured a state championship in football in 1965. The Wildcats went on to capture a fourth state championship in 1977—a feat that never would have happened if not for the Miracle Game of 1977.

New subdivisions began to crop up like mushrooms; schools and libraries were added to meet the growing demand. In 1970, Herbert Hunt announced plans for a new $500 million, 3,959-acre business and residential development in North Texas, with the majority of the property falling within the city limits of Plano.

In 1976, a man named Tino Trujillo arrived in town and soon established his reputation for serving the best Mexican food in Plano. But his biggest accomplishment came almost ten years later, when he helped found Collin County Community College, now Collin College.

Also in 1976, a young man named John Herrington graduated from Plano Senior High School; he went on to became the first Native American in space.

In 1979, Ross Perot announced that Electronic Data Systems (EDS) had purchased nearly two thousand acres of land, signaling its plans to relocate corporate headquarters to Plano and the beginnings of the Legacy Business Park. As the 1980s dawned, more big change was on the horizon.

EXPLOSIVE GROWTH (1980–2000)

Population in 2000: 222,030

The last two decades of the twentieth century saw explosive growth in Plano, with EDS, Frito-Lay, JCPenney and other large companies moving their headquarters here. Plano's population grew tenfold, transforming a bedroom community to a large city. Collin Creek Mall opened in 1981. In 1995, the President George Bush Highway opened, providing an east–west connection across Plano. Another major road, the North Dallas Tollway, extended into Plano, connecting the west side to Dallas.

As the population grew, so did Plano ISD. In 1980, the system had more than twenty-two thousand students and seventeen elementary schools, five middle schools and three high schools; many more school buildings were added in the next twenty years.

All this explosive growth had a dark side. Fourteen Plano teenagers committed suicide from 1983 to 1984. Between 1996 and 1997, eleven young people in Plano died of heroin overdoses. Both episodes thrust the city into the national spotlight, portraying Plano as a poster city for suburban dystopia.

With the heroin epidemic, the community mobilized to educate teens, and law enforcement went after the dealers. Near the end of 1997, Plano police announced the arrest of the city's biggest heroin supplier.

In the late 1990s, with construction for the DART light commuter rail underway, downtown Plano began to enjoy a renaissance.

RECENT YEARS (2000–PRESENT)

Population, 2016 (estimated): 286,057

Recent years have brought continued and explosive growth in Plano, with the arrival of corporate and regional headquarters for Toyota, FedEx Office, Liberty Mutual, JP Morgan Chase and Boeing. Legacy Town Center added shops and restaurants, followed by development of Legacy West. DART light rail service opened in Plano in 2002, accelerating the renaissance of downtown.

Plano witnessed not only massive growth in population but also significant changes in demographics. The arrival of corporate headquarters brought professionals from around the world and boosted the city's diversity. In 1980, Plano was more than 90 percent Anglo; by the 2010 census, about 55 percent of Plano's population was Anglo, 19 percent Asian, 15 percent Hispanic and 8 percent African American.

Through all these changes, a committed group of Plano citizens worked diligently to preserve Plano's history. The Plano Conservancy for Historic Preservation was established in 2001, and the Interurban Railway Museum opened in 2003.

Plano's Oldest Tree

Located in the southeast section of Bob Woodruff Park, a stone marks Plano's Bicentennial Bur Oak Tree as the oldest tree in the city of Plano. However, it turns out that "Bicentennial" was a bit of a misnomer.

When the marker was placed at the foot of the tree in 1987, experts estimated its age at about two hundred years old, based on the field dating technology available at the time. However, more recent estimates using laboratory technology suggest the tree is at least five hundred years old.

That means the tree was there to witness the buffalo that gathered at Rowlett Creek for water and the Caddo Indians who farmed in the area. The tree was there when the Prince brothers explored the area and the Albritton family enjoyed the property for camping and Scout activities. During the early settlement of Plano, the land was cleared for firewood and fence posts, but again, the tree was spared.

Before the land became a city park, previous owners included the Dr. Daniel Rowlett family, Colonel Landon W. Oglesby, the William T. Land family, William D. Prince and the Claude C. Albritton family. The Land family used the timber on the property for their west Plano farm, but somehow, the bur oak tree was spared.

Bur oak trees are generally found along stream bottoms and adjacent slopes in North and East Central Texas. Plano's Bicentennial Bur Oak is no exception; it is situated in a section of Bob Woodruff Park known as "bottomland." Because the area has been prone to flooding, no private

The Bicentennial Bur Oak in Bob Woodruff Park has a crown spread of eighty feet. *Photo by Mary Jacobs.*

structures were ever built on the property. Rich sediment brought in from other areas by heavy rains and flooding helped nourish the tree.

Bur oak wood is heavy, hard, impermeable and durable, and the trees are very hardy, tolerating drought and city pollution. The thick, corky bark enables the bur oak tree to withstand fire and other damage better

A plaque marks the oldest tree in Plano.

than most oaks. The tree provides deep shade and has few insect or disease problems. In winter, the corky twigs and stout branches give bur oak trees a picturesque appearance, and their large acorns provide tasty snacks for wildlife.

The tree at Bob Woodruff Park was designated the Bicentennial Bur Oak Tree in 1987, in recognition of the tree's existence at the time of the signing of the U.S. Constitution. Experts used a tool called an increment borer to estimate the tree's age at around two hundred years old. (The tool takes out a core sample thinner than a pencil. One can then see the number of annual rings per inch in the sample, multiply the number by the tree's trunk radius and arrive at a ballpark estimate of its age.)

In February 2002, the tree was registered with the Dallas Historic Tree Coalition and measured at approximately ninety feet tall, 186 inches in circumference and with a crown spread of eighty feet. The citizens of Plano celebrated the life of the tree and recognized the history of the land surrounding it at Plano's 2002 Arbor Day Celebration.

In 2006, a large branch broke off the tree, and the tree was re-aged by Dr. Harold Arnott, a dean and professor of the University of Texas–Arlington's Biology Department. "A sample 'tree cookie' was taken from the fallen branch, examined under an electron microscope and estimated at 226 years old," according to Renée Burke Jordan, AICP, park planning manager for the City of Plano. "Extrapolating from that data and using trunk measurements, Dr. Arnott estimated the tree's total age at more than 500 years old."

So it turns out Plano's oldest tree is even older than originally believed. Likely it was there well before the signing of the U.S. Constitution. The tree may have sprouted not long after Columbus sailed across the ocean and presided over the land that is now Plano long before Europeans settled the New World.

Next time you're at Bob Woodruff Park, head for the southeast corner and check out the magnificent Bicentennial Bur Oak—or, perhaps more accurately, the Quincentennial Bur Oak![4]

HENRY COOK

War of 1812 Veteran

N owadays, we marvel when someone embarks on a challenging new adventure after the age of seventy, and we credit modern advances in medical care, health and nutrition for making that possible. That makes Henry Cook's story so amazing. He was in his seventies when he took on a daunting task: leading a caravan of settlers from Illinois to Texas in 1846.

Not only did Cook become one of Plano's earliest Anglo settlers—arriving here just as Texas was entering statehood—he also ranks among its oldest. Born on the eve of the Revolutionary War and a veteran of the War of 1812, Henry Cook established himself as the patriarch of a clan with descendants still living in Plano today. And at least two key institutions in Plano—a church that's active today and a cemetery in the middle of the Shops of Legacy—continue to bear witness to Henry Cook's remarkable life story.

A LIFE ON THE FRONTIER

Having spent most of his life on the frontier, Henry Cook certainly had the know-how to help settle the "wild waste" that was the Collin County area at the time.[5]

He was born on May 28, 1775, in Fincastle, Castle County, in what is now West Virginia. Soon after, his parents moved to Green County, Illinois, where they lived in Kaskaskia,[6] a French settlement near a Native American village.

A small plaque in the ground honors Henry Cook's service in the War of 1812. *Find-a-Grave.com*.

Cook served in the War of 1812 as a French and Native American interpreter, eventually achieving the rank of lieutenant. (He is one of only two War of 1812 veterans buried in Plano; Thomas Finley, the other, is buried in Young Cemetery.) Military records indicate that he served two stints as a "Mounted Spy"—first in Captain Samuel Judy's company in the Illinois Militia and later in Captain Samuel Whiteside's Company of Mounted Rangers. Likely these life experiences prepared Cook to become a Texas pioneer. Certainly, he learned how to find his way around in the wilderness and survive.

Life on the frontier was never easy. North Texas was largely unsettled. Some feeble attempts had been made to start settlements, but "they were scarcely more than widely separated dots on the boundless prairie."[7]

Cook had four wives over the course of his lifetime and apparently outlived three of them.[8] When he arrived in Texas, he was accompanied by his fourth wife, Sarah "Sally" Kincaid, and their six children, as well as many of the six grown children from his previous marriage. All of his children by those two marriages eventually settled in Denton and Collin Counties, within a day's ride of Henry Cook's home.

A GRUELING JOURNEY

According to *Plano, Texas: The Early Years*, "Henry was evidently a man of forceful and magnetic personality to the end of his days. He led a caravan from Illinois to Texas at the age of 75, a task seldom undertaken by any but a younger man."

It's almost impossible to truly appreciate how grueling that journey must have been, especially for a man in his seventies. The pioneers would have spent long days on the trail in a wagon. As nighttime neared, they would pitch a camp and build a fire. The next morning, they'd have to pack everything up again and return to the trail. The threats of wild animals and raiding parties of Native American tribes were always present. Staples and supplies were limited to what could be packed on the wagon. Disease or injuries, easily treated today, could quickly become life-threatening. Trail and way-markers were few. And of course, the entire journey was accomplished without benefit of motorized transport, climate control or GoreTex.

Cook first led the caravan to St. Louis, Missouri, where they secured a waybill: a ticket to a vehicle, probably a wagon drawn by oxen, to carry the family and their goods to Texas. This was necessary because there were no roads and the Mississippi River could only be crossed in certain places with wagon and oxen. In St. Louis, the party purchased a cook stove and some tools, including a froe (cleaving tool) for making shingles and a broadax to square logs.

On October 15, 1846, the caravan reached Trinity Mills.[9] However, Cook thought this area too low and wet to be healthy, so after a couple of weeks, he moved the group to an area called Old Indian Springs, where they camped in a tent for the winter. In the spring, the settlers established permanent residence near the area where the Shops of Legacy is now located. Cook selected property in two separate tracts and began the process of obtaining deeds as a Peters Colonist. Henry Cook's log home was situated on 320 acres of fertile prairie. The other 320-acre parcel was poor land, but it furnished ample wood and water.

Texas in Henry Cook's Time

While Henry Cook was one of the first settlers in the Plano area, he was one of thousands venturing to Texas for adventure and opportunity around the same time. From a population of about 20,000 in 1830, Texas grew to over 140,000 hardy frontier settlers by the late 1840s. In 1835, honorary Texas frontiersman Davy Crockett uttered his famous directive, "You may all go to hell and I will go to Texas." Whether following Crockett's example or following their own dreams, thousands of people did just that. They up and went to Texas.[10] When Cook arrived, Texas had just been admitted (December 29, 1845) as the twenty-eighth state, although at that time "Texas" comprised the present state of Texas as well as parts of New Mexico, Colorado and Wyoming. Texas was admitted with the provision that the area (389,166 square miles) should be divided into no more than five states "of convenient size." The first Texas state government was formally installed in Austin, with J. Pinckney Henderson taking the oath of office as governor, on February 19, 1846. Around the same time, the first skirmishes that would lead to the Mexican-American War were underway near the border.[11]

Things were more peaceful in North Texas, but there was much work to do. For any newly arrived settlers, the first order of business was to build a permanent shelter. Henry Cook and his family initially built two log cabins. Later, one large room was constructed with a white rock chimney, known as a dirt and stick chimney.

Like most early Texas settlers, Henry Cook and his fellow settlers likely spent most of their time doing backbreaking labor from sunup to sundown, as the website of the Bullock Museum in Austin describes:

> *Crops had to be planted, tended, and harvested. Chickens, pigs, cows, and goats required care. Daily food had to be hunted and caught. The frontier provided no linen or lace, so women sewed tanned deer hide into buckskin clothing. Those lucky few who had managed to strap a spinning wheel onto their wagons before leaving their U.S. homes spun their own cotton to make less pungent and heavy clothing. Any kind of trade with the other far-flung Texas settlements required weeks of hazardous travel on dirt track roads. Settlers organized home schooling and church services, although both were haphazard and occasional experiences. For most settlers, rest and recreation, like coffee and cigarettes, were usually in short supply but greatly enjoyed when available.*[12]

The four daughters of Henry and Sarah Kincaid Cook. *Left to right*: Martha Martin, Elizabeth Heustis, Rachel Baccus and Sara Dudley. *Plano Public Library, Plano, Texas.*

Cook went to work to establish his herd of cattle. Using money from the sale of his farm in Illinois, he traveled east to purchase one hundred head of cattle and then used the final installment on the farm to purchase additional cattle.

Life was especially hard and isolated for women who followed their husbands to the frontier, perhaps reluctantly. "Men talked hopefully of the future; children reveled in the novelty of the present; but the women—ah, there was where the situation bore heaviest," wrote Noah Smithwick in 1830. "As one old lady remarked, Texas is heaven for men and dogs, but a hell for women and oxen. They—the women—talked sadly of the old homes and friends left behind, so very far behind it seemed then, of the hardships and bitter privations they were undergoing and the dangers that surrounded them."

The possibility of attacks by Native Americans struck cold fear in the hearts of the settlers. On one occasion, Native Americans appeared near the Cooks' log cabin, and Henry's wife, Sarah, reportedly grabbed a pot of steaming beans and set it outside the cabin's animal skin door to appease the visitors. "She breathed freely only when they ate the beans and drove off with a yearling, but harmed no one," according to the account.[13]

By 1854, the Shawnee Trail was established as an important cattle route between Brownsville, Texas, and Kansas City. Henry Cook's home was located on a little crest so that it was visible in all directions, becoming a trail marker by day and a lighthouse at night. The Cook house became a bit of a legend, known as "the lonesome house" due to its location. It was also a popular gathering point for neighbors who came to dance.[14]

TRAGEDY STRIKES

Within a few months of the Cook family's arrival, tragedy struck. Henry Cook's seventeen-year-old son, Daniel, died on January 13, 1847. He was buried on a plot of land not far from the Cook cabin, which eventually became Baccus Cemetery. Today, the cemetery remains, a quiet spot in the middle of the Shops of Legacy. Daniel's grave is believed to be the first marked grave in Collin County.

Unfortunately, death was a fact of life for pioneers, especially for infant children. The next burial was one of Henry Cook's grandchildren: George W. Martin, son of J.B. and Martha Cook Martin, Henry's eldest child with Sarah Kincaid Cook. George was only sixteen months old when he died on August 17, 1850, and was buried next to his uncle Daniel.

In time, Henry Cook's daughter Rachel Baccus acquired the land where the cemetery is located, and in 1878, she deeded it to the heirs of Henry Cook for church and cemetery purposes. In about 1915, the cemetery association changed the name to Baccus Cemetery in recognition of Rachel's gift of the burial ground and the tract for the neighboring Baccus Christian Church, organized in 1908. A cemetery board is responsible for the cemetery, which has about 285 marked graves; an endowment fund provides income for maintenance. A Texas State Historical Marker stands at the gate. Among the families buried at Baccus Cemetery who are descended from Henry Cook are the Cook, Heustis, Martin, Dudley, Baccus, Miller, Bishop and Pearson families. One of the last burials was that of Libby Louise Pearson, twenty-three, in 1979, a sixth-generation descendant of Henry Cook. (There is still ongoing disagreement over the name of the cemetery; in honor of its original owner, Henry Cook, some think it should be known as the "Cook Baccus Cemetery.")

Descendants of Henry Cook still live in Plano and Collin County, and a few of them are still farming. The Baccus farm was recognized by the Texas Department of Agriculture for inclusion in the Family Land Heritage Registry as one of the farms that had been operated by the same family for over one hundred years.

Another part of Henry Cook's legacy, still visible in Plano, is a church that he helped found. Along with his eldest son, John Cook, Henry was a charter member of Liberty Baptist Church. Records show that the church met in "the lonesome house" for some time before a dedicated building was erected. That congregation—now named Willow Bend Church—is still active today and celebrated its 160th anniversary in 2010.[15]

DEATH

In 1862, the remarkable life of Henry Cook came to an end when he died at the age of eighty-seven.

One historian described the story of Peters Colony as "a story of hardships and dangers, but also a story of courage and faith, of hard work and achievement, resulting in settling one of the most fertile areas of the state."[16]

The last inning of Henry Cook's life mirrors that story. Despite his relatively advanced age, he led his family and others as they settled the blackland soil of Plano—considered some of the best and richest in North Texas, perhaps even in the United States. He helped create incredible opportunity and prosperity for his family, and his contributions are still benefiting the residents of Plano today.

If you've ever visited Willow Bend Church, you can thank the faith and vision of Henry Cook. If you ever pause for a quiet moment at Baccus Cemetery, you can thank Henry Cook for his contribution to Plano in its formative years. And you can pause to take a moment to look for his tombstone, which reads:

COOK, Lieut. Henry Cook, born May 28, 1775 Died June 10, 1862.

"Take him, O Father, in thine arms, and may he henceforth be a messenger of peace between our human hearts and thee." "We only know that thou hast gone, and that the same relent-less tide which bore thee from us, still glides on, and we who mourn thee with it glide." "I fear not death"

Headstone for Lieutenant Henry Cook. *Find-a-Grave.com.*

COLLINWOOD CORNERSTONE MYSTERY

E verybody loves a good mystery. When a mystery emerged after the city took possession of the Collinwood House sometime around 2014, a team of investigators went to work and cracked the case. The "mystery" was a stone in the hearth of the parlor of the Collinwood House, hand-inscribed with the words "James A. Bell 1861."

The discovery had preservationists scratching their heads. No James Bell had ever owned the home or lived in it. Who was he? And why was his name inscribed on this limestone rock in such a prominent place in this historic home?

PRIVATE HOME

The house now known as the Collinwood House sat on private land for more than 150 years, a living legacy of Plano's pioneer heritage hidden from public view. It was built by brothers C.M. and J.K. Fox, probably around 1861. A year later, in 1862, the Fox brothers sold the land and the house to Clinton Shepard Haggard and his wife, Nancy Katherine (Lunsford) Haggard. The Haggard family owned the house until the late 1930s.

The land and house changed hands a few more times until 2009, when the City of Plano purchased eighty acres along Windhaven Drive for use as a city park. After the tenants vacated the home, sometime around 2014,

Above: The "mystery" inscription discovered inside the Collinwood House. *Photo by Candace Fountoulakis.*

Left: The stone, shown in the hearth next to the stairwell in the main sitting room of the Collinwood House. *Photo by Amy Sandling Crawford.*

Plano preservationists got a first peek inside the structure, and that's when they spotted the stone inscribed by James A. Bell. Three residents—Candace Fountoulakis, John Brooks and Marianne Wells—along with others, started digging into old historic records and finally found the answer.

James A Bell was a "freighter"—a hauler of goods—at the time the house was built by the Fox brothers. He hailed from Tennessee and married Rhoda Elizabeth Brown in Collin County in 1856. As a freighter or "teamster," Bell hauled supplies by wagon to the frontier that is now the western portion of Plano.

Before the railroad arrived in Plano in 1872, supplies like pine boards for flooring and cypress for siding were transported by wagon from East Texas. There were no local mills to produce sawn boards for homebuilding, so pioneers had to have the lumber hauled in, most frequently from Jefferson, Texas.

Milled boards were discovered under the exterior shingles of the Collinwood House. *Photo by Candace Fountoulakis.*

Bell was just such a hauler. According to diaries of the day, the area where the house was built by the Fox brothers in 1861 was referred to as "White Rock" for the abundant limestone along the nearby creek. Beneath the house built on thick hand-hewn oak logs were white rock boulders.

Because of the shingles on the outside of the house, many had assumed the house was built much later. But the research into Bell's identity and history led to clues suggesting that the house was built much earlier—probably during the first year of the Civil War.

Under those shingles were milled boards that formed the original exterior cladding of the house built by the Fox brothers. The shingles had acted as a weather barrier and actually preserved the clapboards. Hand-forged square nails and wooden pegs secured siding and foundation beams to form a rock-solid structure. Wide pine floors throughout the house are studded with the same antique nails.

Furthermore, the boulders beneath the house and the inscribed fireplace rock are emblematic of the 1860s, as is a log discovered, bark intact, in a load-bearing wall along the cellar stairs. (The cellar itself is a rarity for the region and may represent an enlargement of a primitive dugout, excavated before construction of the house.) One former resident reported seeing Bell's cornerstone in the house's cellar; apparently the stone was moved to the fireplace surround during a renovation in the 1940s.

Bell likely helped haul the lumber to the building site for the home and perhaps helped build it too. Whatever his involvement, it seems he wanted to leave his mark—his name—in the cornerstone of the original house.

JAMES A. BELL

Bell's history doesn't end with the Fox/Haggard house. He and his family moved to Denton County, as did the Fox brothers. Fox Avenue in Lewisville is named for their influential families. Rhoda Brown Bell's nephew was George Pearis Brown, an attorney in McKinney and author of histories of early Collin County. Relatives of Rhoda's from the Brown, Russell and Beverly families are buried in pioneer cemeteries in Plano.

The Bells left Denton County and headed west to Montague County, burying their son James there when he died at age thirteen. Rhoda and James lived their last years in what is now a ghost town of Indian Territory, which became part of Garvin County, Oklahoma. Their grave

Moving the Collinwood House in 2018. *Photo by Candace Fountoulakis.*

markers are hidden in the overgrown plots of Old Purdy Cemetery west of Pauls Valley.

In 2018, the house of Clinton Shepard and Nannie Kate Haggard was relocated from its original location to a spot half a mile northwest near where C.S. Haggard's first home was located in the 1850s. Television news helicopters hovered overhead as a team from Lemons House Moving carefully lifted the house onto wheeled dollies and inched it along Windhaven Drive to its new location.

The limestone boulders from beneath the house were salvaged and will complement the Bell rock as part of a restoration plan. The house will be fully restored to showcase a glimpse into the frontier past of Plano.

No doubt, there are more secrets still held within the walls of the Collinwood House—but they will not be a hidden part of Plano's history for much longer.

MULE CAPITAL OF THE WORLD

Today, Plano is known as home to a number of international corporations. But 150 years ago, Plano had a different claim to fame: Mule Capital of the World.

In the fall of 1866, Collin County was the leading mule market west of the Mississippi. General Sheridan sent purchasing agents here to supply mules for the Northern armies.

Even with improved machinery, mulepower and horsepower were the engines of the agricultural industry at the time. Mules were so profitable that everyone in Plano, even the barber and the postman, took to trading them. But for a few of Plano's founding fathers, mules weren't just a sideline; they were big business.

A bit of explanation for those of us who are city slickers: a mule is a cross between a male donkey (a jack) and a female horse (a mare.) Plano's business got started with C.S. Haggard, who hauled a jack from Kentucky behind his covered wagon when he traveled to Texas in 1858. That jack was so big that he was nicknamed "Mammoth Jack" and went on to sire a strain that made mule history in Texas. "Plano mules" were known for their size, strength and endurance. The mules were often sold in matching pairs—roughly equal in size and strength so that they could pull well together—and a good pair went for $600 or more.

Mules were also very smart. One pioneer physician, Dr. Dye, rode many miles in the course of his doctoring. Often, on his way home at night, he was bone tired. It was said that he could trust his mule to carry him home

J.W. Shepard Mule Barn. *Plano Public Library, Plano, Texas.*

safely, even if he fell sound asleep and arrived home with snow and icicles in his beard.

By 1871, C.S. had 207 horses and mules, reportedly more than anyone else in the country, and was a frequent prize winner at the county fair. But it was his son-in-law J.W. Shepard who took the business to yet another level. J.W. Shepard owned a 2,200-acre ranch on what is now Plano's east side. (The remnants of the corral used to load and unload the mules remained in what is now Heritage Ranch Golf & Country Club, a housing development in Fairview, until 2009, when the community built a replica of the old corral at the same location.) J.W. began transporting mules by the carload from Missouri and shipped mules not only out of the county and state but as far away as Mexico, South America and Honduras.

To serve the trade coming and going by railroad, J.W. operated a mule barn, located at what is now Avenue J between 14th and 15th Streets. (A historic marker can be spotted on the sidewalk near the Masonic Lodge.) J.W. helped establish Second Monday Trade Days in Plano and for half a century was a familiar figure on the lot. During those years, many people in Plano awoke in the morning to the sounds of mules braying in his barn and pens.

Trades Day at the Jockey Yard. *Plano Public Library, Plano, Texas.*

Mammoth Jack, a modern metal sculpture, reminds visitors at the DART Rail station of Plano's past distinction as Mule Capital of the World. *Photo by Mary Jacobs.*

Many other farmers in Plano raised and sold mules, including the Carpenters, the Rasors, the Haggards and the Gregorys, but J.W. had the largest and most widely visible operation. "J.W. became known for his fine livestock which he developed as a means of realizing the full potential of the land he so deeply loved," according to *Plano: The Early Years*. He also served on the school board and Plano City Council. When he died at the age of ninety in 1946, the *Dallas News* wrote: "Probably no other man has ever done so much for Plano and South Collin, furnished work to more people and fed more hungry less fortunate people than has J.W. Shepard."[17]

Shepard Elementary is named after J.W. Shepard—the man who did so much for Plano, including helping the city earn its nickname, Mule Capital of the World.

Wells in Downtown Plano

Fires were a constant threat in downtown Plano in the city's early years. To provide water for firefighting, the city council ordered a well dug in September 1890 at the intersection of 15th Street and Avenue K (then known as Main and Mechanic). The well cost $225 and was completed on December 1, 1890. The well was locked and used for city purposes, according to the minutes of city council from September 8, 1890, and November 19, 1890. Other wells were later dug throughout downtown.

According to a brief newspaper item (date unknown), "Years ago Plano was referred to as The City of Wells as were many villages where the only source of water was from wells."

The Sanborn Map from 1896 on the following page shows the locations of several wells in the downtown Plano area. This map was created by the Sanborn Map Company, which published detailed maps of U.S. cities and towns in the nineteenth and twentieth centuries in order for fire insurance companies to assess liabilities.

Many businesses located in older buildings, as well as historic homes, in the downtown area still have wells to this day, although most are sealed and no longer in use.

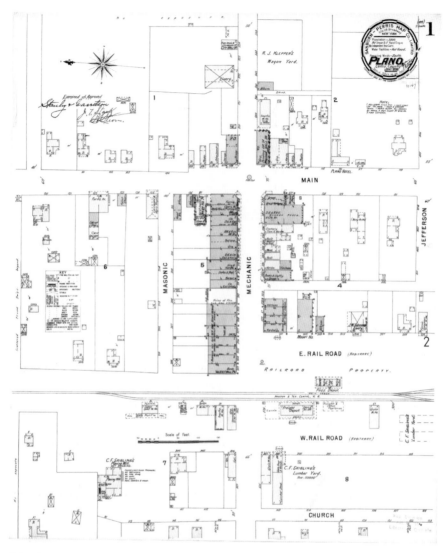

A Sanborn Map shows the location of the wells dug in downtown Plano. *Library of Congress, Geography and Map Division.*

DEATH IS A SALESMAN

Today, Preston Lakes is a quiet, manicured neighborhood in an affluent area of Plano. Almost 120 years ago, it was the site of one of Plano's darkest hours.

Imagine two men working under cover of darkness on an isolated patch of farmland. They toiled at night, believing that would reduce the chance of infection. Their grim task: burying the body of an eleven-year-old girl, a member of the Collinsworth family.

The men weren't just grieving. They were terrified. Who would die next?

The little girl was the first victim in a smallpox outbreak that ultimately killed fifteen and rocked the community of Plano in 1895.

"It was a scary time," said Charlotte Carpenter Johnson, an Allen resident and descendant of the family. "They had to bury the dead very quickly."

KILLER HOSPITALITY

The sad saga began days earlier, when, following frontier custom, the family of Daniel M. "Milt" Collinsworth welcomed a traveling peddler into the home. "Unfortunately, the family's hospitality ended up being their demise," said Plano preservation advocate Candace Fountoulakis.

At the time, Plano was a small community of just 1,300 souls; the extended Collinsworth family owned large portions of what is now west

Collinsworth Cemetery was established in 1895 due to a smallpox epidemic. *Photo by Mary Jacobs.*

Plano. They were farmers from Tennessee and Virginia and relatives of James Collinsworth, a signer of the Texas Declaration of Independence.

When the peddler left the next morning, he mentioned that he felt unwell. The chore of changing his bed linens fell to one of Milt's daughters. Within a few days, she fell ill and died soon after. Inexperienced with the disease, the community's doctor misdiagnosed her ailment.

Family members traveled from Allen and Frisco for the funeral. It was a dreary, rainy day, so mourners crowded into the home, with the windows shut. Silently, the deadly disease spread.

Ms. Johnson is the great-great-granddaughter of Farwick Collinsworth, the family patriarch. "Within a matter of weeks," she said, "Farwick lost his wife, two sons, a nephew and at least three grandchildren."

Farwick's wife, Lucy Ann Collinsworth, sixty-four, died next, followed by two of their sons, Levi, thirty-seven, and Ishmel, twenty-five; and two more grandchildren, Mary, three, and Robert, ten. Tobe Collinsworth, twenty-three, a nephew visiting from Kentucky, also died. Other names are lost to history, but Johnson, who researched the Collinsworth family extensively, believes about fifteen ultimately perished. (Smallpox was highly contagious; it could be transmitted through the air, as well as through direct contact with infected bodily fluids or contaminated objects, such as bedding.)

McKinney's newspaper, the *Democrat*, printed a resolution by the Collin County Alliance expressing sympathy: "The family of Brother F.M. Collinsworth of Haggard Alliance have been terribly afflicted by the visitation of smallpox in his family resulting in the death of several family members....Therefore, be it resolved that we tender to the surviving members our heartfelt sympathy in their sore bereavement."

ARMED QUARANTINE

Settlers in the area quickly realized that they needed to do more than extend sympathy. They needed to take action to stop the spread of disease.

On May 6, 1895, Plano City Council called an emergency meeting, requiring vaccinations and establishing a strict quarantine "to protect our citizens from this loathsome disease." Anyone within the area between what is now Spring Creek Parkway, Park Boulevard, Coit and Preston Roads was forbidden to leave. An armed guard patrolled the border.

For those within the quarantine, food supplies were limited. One survivor, a man named Bob Fortner, later vowed that he'd never eat rice again, having relied on it for so many meals during this time.

A few brave souls endeavored to assist. One smallpox survivor, Albert Garrett, nursed the sick. Silas Harrington, owner of a pharmacy downtown, delivered groceries to the quarantine line.

History leaves us no details on the traveling salesman, but he likely was part of a chain of transmission that had gradually carried the disease toward Plano. An epidemic had ravaged Brooklyn, New York, from 1892 to 1894, triggering panic and riots. Patients with smallpox experience a sudden onset of high fever, malaise, headaches, body aches and sometimes vomiting. The rash does not appear until after two to four days, which may explain the doctor's initial misdiagnosis of the Collinsworth girl.

A Peaceful Monument

Oddly, Johnson never heard about the epidemic until stumbling across a newspaper article. She thinks the memory was too painful for the family. "The Collinsworth family had a stigma on them for many years afterward," she said. "Their neighbors were frightened and avoided them."

Happily, however, the story concludes on a note of healing. The outbreak established Collinsworth Cemetery, which now occupies a quiet spot between two homes near Parker and Ohio Roads. Once forgotten, it now occupies a beautifully landscaped lot in the neighborhood.

When Johnson learned of the graveyard's existence in the late 1980s, it was in disrepair. But one by one, community groups stepped in to help. Toll Brothers provided the fence, the Fulbright family donated the entrance sign and Plano Conservancy added a wayside marker. Preston Lakes HOA, Boy Scouts and master gardeners pitched in with landscaping and other projects. Johnson formed a 501c nonprofit association to manage the property. (The family owns the graveyard in perpetuity.)

Headstone at Collinsworth Cemetery. *Photo by Mary Jacobs.*

"It was really an amazing cooperative effort," she said. "I couldn't begin to list all of the people who have helped."

When the development opened, some of the first buyers in the area opted for properties right next door to the cemetery. As they saw it, they were getting a home next to a park—and neighbors they could count on to be very quiet.

Now, anyone can enjoy the serene spot and visit the graves of Lucy, Ishmel and Levy, whose headstone calls him "a loving husband, a dear father, a faithful friend."

"The cemetery went from being a swampy, muddy mess…to a beautiful place of renewal and hope," said Fountoulakis. "I think that's exactly how the family would want it to be represented."

ABOUT SMALLPOX

Prior to the wide availability of the vaccine, smallpox was one of the most feared diseases on the planet. It was extremely contagious and killed and disfigured millions. A 1988 article in the *American Journal of Public Health* described the havoc wreaked by this horrific disease:

> *Imagine what it would be like if you could get AIDS by simply standing near an infected person at work, in school, in a hospital or anywhere else; if you had a chance of dying of one in four if you did get it.…Imagine that when you did contract the disease it would transform you into a hideous monster, rack your body with constant pain, and cause your family and friends to fear and shun you—some perceiving your illness as evidence of divine wrath.*[18]

Plano's outbreak occurred almost one hundred years after Edward Jenner discovered the smallpox vaccine in 1796. (Jenner never made a profit; he chose not to patent the vaccine because he believed it should be available for all.) The smallpox vaccination was introduced in the United States in 1800; however, tragically for the Collinsworth family and others on the frontier, it likely wasn't easy to obtain. Some were fearful or suspicious of the vaccine. While it was effective in reducing the spread of disease, state-imposed vaccination programs met with resistance from the beginning.

The pioneers likely contracted the variola major type, with a fatality rate of 20 to 50 percent, according to Daphne Lynch, an epidemiologist with Collin County Health Care Services. Even those who survived suffered for the rest of their lives. Some were blinded. Young women whose faces were horribly disfigured found their marriage prospects evaporate overnight. In Europe, some smallpox survivors committed suicide or entered convents.

In 1895, the year smallpox struck Plano, two major milestones in the disease's history also occurred. They illustrate how disparities in the adoption of the vaccine became a matter of life and death. Sweden, the first country to adopt Jenner's vaccine, announced the eradication of smallpox in that country in 1895. The same year, the town of Gloucester, England, was struck by a smallpox epidemic that ultimately killed 434 people.

England had required vaccination for all babies since 1853, but that law sparked the world's first anti-vaccination societies, publications and rallies. "The state has no right to encroach upon parental responsibility, or to impose either religious or medical dogmas upon the people of this country on any pretense whatever," wrote William Tebb, president of the London Society for the Abolition of Compulsory Vaccination, in 1887.[19]

A wave of anti-vaccination feeling took root in Gloucester, with several officials elected for their opposition of "Jennerism" and their promises not to prosecute those who opted out of vaccination. Gloucester became the least-vaccinated county in the country, with 83 percent of the population failing to comply with the law. Then the horror began. Perhaps because of the political debate, many photographs still exist documenting the terrible effects of the disease.

A mass vaccination effort ultimately put the outbreak under control, but not before almost two thousand people were infected, two-thirds of them children under age ten. The Gloucester outbreak—which, ironically, took place less than twenty miles from the spot where Jenner developed the vaccine—was Britain's last great smallpox epidemic.

Smallpox was declared eradicated in 1979 by the World Health Organization.

A Lodge and a Museum

T o become historic, a building has to stand the test of time and overcome multiple threats and obstacles. Many buildings are lost to fire, tornadoes, earthquakes and even developers before they have a chance to become historically significant.

Downtown Plano is lucky to have numerous historic buildings, including two that have been adapted and repurposed as museums. Most people are familiar with the Interurban Railway Museum, but downtown has another, lesser-known museum: the North Texas Masonic Historical Museum and Library, located on the first floor of the Plano Masonic Lodge.

Just off 15th Street at 1414 J Avenue, behind McCall Plaza and adjacent to the Fillmore Pub, the building that houses the museum was originally known as the Moore House Hotel. It was built in 1898, replacing the original Moore House that was destroyed in the devastating fire of 1895.

The book *Plano, Texas: The Early Days* offers a passage from the diary of Mrs. C.S. Haggard describing the fire. Haggard documented not only the destruction of the original Moore House but also the burning of Bowser Skiles Implement & Opera, a dry goods store, two saddler shops, a furniture store, two grocery stores and the National Bank, including the bank's upper story, which housed the offices of Plano professionals.

The Moore House provided respite for weary travelers on the Houston and Texas Central Railroad, located where DART tracks now run. The railroad depot was located at the present site of McCall Plaza, making the Moore House a convenient place to spend the night. Due to the hotel's

Exterior of the Masonic Lodge in downtown Plano. *Photo by Jennifer Shertzer,* Plano Magazine.

The North Texas Masonic Historical Museum and Library is open to the public on the first floor of the Masonic Lodge. *Photo by Jennifer Shertzer,* Plano Magazine.

proximity to the railroad depot, folk tales persist that sex workers used the Moore House for a home base. Research could neither confirm nor "put to bed" these salacious rumors.

The building was eventually purchased in August 1924 by the Plano Masonic Lodge for $5,000 from J.W. and Molly Shepard. A visitor to the building will notice the date of 1925 at the top of the façade along with the lodge number, 768. A significant year for the building is 1925, when the front porch was removed and exterior stucco added. That year also represents the date that the building became the permanent home of the Plano Masonic Lodge.

The Lodge operates the North Texas Masonic Historical Museum and Library and is open to the public every Monday, Wednesday and Friday from 1:00 to 4:00 p.m. and closed on holidays. The library contains almost two thousand historical and Masonic books. The museum preserves archives and collections not only of North Texas Masonic history but also the rich history of Plano, Collin County and North Texas.

MILLINERY IN PLANO

I n the late nineteenth century, no fine lady left her home without a hat. Hats were not just fashionable; they were essential. Society ladies cultivated milliners and expected them to come up with unique and exquisite designs. And they jealously kept their sources secret.

You might guess that, in the 1890s, a young woman in a small town like Plano would need to travel to a big city—or at least to Dallas—to find beautiful hats like the ones modeled in these photos. A place known as the "Mule Capital of the World" might not seem like a mecca for elegant ladies' hats, but in fact, there were milliners working in Plano who may have supplied those fashion fixes. (A "milliner" is a person who designs,

Plano residents loved their hats. Records identify these ladies, *left to right*, as Frankie C., Ada Smith, Maggie C. and Alice Taylor, 1897. *Plano Public Library, Plano, Texas.*

Maude Goode, a Plano resident, probably early twentieth century. *Plano Public Library, Plano, Texas.*

makes, trims or sells women's hats.) Written records suggest that at least four women in Plano worked as milliners in the late nineteenth and early twentieth centuries.

Sidney Johnson Mathews owned the Mathews Department Store from 1895 until 1947, when the store was bought by Nathan White. Sidney's wife, Nancy, and their daughters, Ollie and Theo, were milliners at least from 1895 until Nancy passed away in 1920. Mattie B. Hulse, who married William S. Muegge in 1902, also worked for the Mathews family.

From 1898 to 1914, Lizzie Smoot kept extensive diaries of daily life in Plano. Her account mentions her niece Mattie Hulse Muegge visiting the Mathewses at the store. Among Mattie's responsibilities that Lizzie detailed: trimming hats, at home and at the store as needed.

THE PLANO NINE BASEBALL TEAM

In 1972, the Washington Senators headed west to Arlington, Texas, and transformed themselves into the Texas Rangers. That was the year that North Texas joined the Major Leagues.

However, baseball has a storied history that goes way back before 1972. The Fort Worth Cats (also known as the Panthers) started in 1884, playing in various leagues up until 2014. During this time, the Cats won sixteen league pennants and won the Dixie Series (a series between the Texas and Southern League champions) eight times between 1920 and 1939.

Dallas had a team in the Texas League from 1902 to 1948 and a team in the Texas Association from 1896 to 1898. The team had numerous nicknames including the Griffins, the Giants, the Marines, the Submarines, the Steers, the Rebels, the Eagles and the Rangers. From 1960 to 1963, the DFW area had a joint team known as the Dallas–Fort Worth Rangers.

By the late nineteenth century, almost every city in North Texas had a baseball team—from the Bonham Bingers to the Paris Red Peppers to the Sherman-Denison Twins. Even Plano had a baseball team, originally known as the Plano Nine.

The year 1897 was a frustrating one for the Plano Nine, as they lost numerous games to their hated rival to the east, the Wylie Shamrocks. Plano baseball devotees had two goals in 1898: build a team that could defeat anyone in Texas and break the trend of losing to the Wylie Shamrocks. One goal would be accomplished while the other would be derailed by forces beyond their control.

The Plano Nine baseball team. *Plano Public Library, Plano, Texas.*

Two baseball players arrived in Plano in 1898 from Kansas looking for a professional opportunity. The players met with Plano alderman Thomas Osgood Ray, who was in the cotton business, and C.E. Hood, who later became one of the directors of the Plano Mutual Cemetery Association. Ray and Hood agreed to manage the team. Three other players were brought down from Kansas, identified in the records only by these one-word names: Morgan, a pitcher; Hester, a centerfielder; and Loose, a second baseman. Nick Hood and Bob Mitchell Howey were the only Plano players on the team. If it took Kansas ballplayers to have a successful team and beat the Wylie Shamrocks, so be it.

In July 1897, a hurricane destroyed Plano's grandstand. A new grandstand and fenced ballpark were built in the V created by the intersection of the Houston & Texas Central and Cotton Belt Railroads. The next year, the Plano Nine took a new name: Ray's Rough Riders, in honor of manager Thomas Osgood Ray and most likely as a tribute to the Rough Riders of the First U.S. Volunteer Cavalry during the Spanish-American War. The Rough Riders had trained in San Antonio in May and made national

BASEBALL.

McKinney base ball club went to Plano Monday and simply mopped up the earth with that town's best base ball talent. Jack Coffey umpired. The score at the conclusion of the game stood 17 to 6, in favor of McKinney. Oliver and Jones, McKinney's battery, ably backed by the rest of our boys, just succeeded in goose-egging the would-be base ball players of our neighboring town eight of the nine innings—that's all. Jones' twirlers couldn't be located even occasionally and though his support, Oliver had never caught him before the Planoites were not in it from start to finish save in the second inning when they were permitted to score their six and only tallies.

The players were:

Plano—	No.	Tallies
E. Lamm, c	1	
M. Hancock, 3 b	0	
C. Overaker, l. f.	0	
H. Gilmer, p	1	
W. Hughston, 2 b	1	
C. Seigling, r. f.	0	
T. Handcock, c. f.	1	
B. Mitchell, s.s.	1	
M. Hood, r. f.	1	
H. Bowman, 1 b	0	
Total	6	

McKinney—	No.	Tallies
B. Boone, 3 b	2	
J. Warden, 1 b	1	
F. Jones, P	1	
H. Barkham, l. f.	3	
G. Oliver, c.	1	
J. Nale, 2 b	2	
P. Burrus, r. f.	3	
Dr. Taylor, c. f.	2	
H. Oates, s. s.	2	
Total	17	

An article from the *McKinney Democrat*, May 23, 1895. *Plano Public Library, Plano, Texas.*

headlines at the Battle of Las Guasimas on June 24, 1898. Under the leadership of Teddy Roosevelt, the Rough Riders would further distinguish themselves at the Battle of San Juan Hill on July 1.

The Spanish-American War started on April 25, 1898, after the sinking of the USS *Maine*. Two months earlier, on February 15, the USS *Maine* had been gently rocking in Cuba's Havana Harbor when the ship suddenly exploded. Of the USS *Maine*'s 262 crew members, 261 were killed; the only survivor was John Bloomer, a right fielder on the USS *Maine*'s baseball team. In December 1897, the USS *Maine* baseball team had defeated the USS *Marblehead* team 18–3, clinching the pennant as the navy baseball champions in a game played in Florida. Following the attack, "Remember the *Maine*! To Hell with Spain!" became the rallying cry heard across the United States. The war would last until August 13, 1898.

With that new moniker, the Plano Rough Riders went on to enact revenge in a scheduled three-game series against their rivals, the Wylie Shamrocks. After two hard-fought games, the series stood at one win apiece. The third game would decide the winner of the series. On June 8, Kansan Morgan took the mound for the Rough Riders, and for six innings he shut out the Shamrocks, with a baserunner going no further than second base. The Rough Riders were able to push across four runs in those same six innings. The crowd was anxious to see if the Rough Riders could hold on for the final three innings. However, the *McKinney Democrat* reported

Roy's Rough Riders Run Over the Shamrocks.

TheWylie Shamrocks and Plano's crack amateur team played the last of a series of three games Wednesday. The games stood "one and one" and a great crowd was out to see who should get the third one. For six innings the Shamrocks battled to get a man across the home plate, but the second base was as far as they could get. and at the end of the sixth inning, seeing a "shut out" staring them in the face, quit the game on a decision on which both agreed. At the end of sixth inning the score stood 4 to 0 in favor of Plano. Batteries: Wylie, Ragsdale (of Oak Cliff team) and Scott. Plano, Morgan and Moore. Umpires, Hood and Oats.

Ball Game.

The Allen Wonders, of Allen, and Ray's Rough Riders, of Plano played a hotly contested game of eleven innings at Rambo's park yesterday afternoon, resulting in a score of 7 to 6 in favor of the Plano team. The playing was pronounced the best that has been seen here this season. This is the first of a series of three games, one of which will be pulled off this afternoon and another tomorrow. Fine games are promised, and good attendance is expected.

Above: An article in the *McKinney Democrat*, July 27, 1898. *Plano Public Library, Plano, Texas.*

Left: An article in the *McKinney Courier-Gazette*, June 9, 1908. *Plano Public Library, Plano, Texas.*

that the Wylie Shamrocks decided to concede the contest after six innings. The Shamrocks must have felt it would have been futile to try to score a run off of ace pitcher Morgan. Plano, with help from the Kansas hired guns, would have revenge on Wylie, winning the series two games to one.

In July, the Rough Riders took on the Allen Wonders. Allen, Texas, was the next stop north of Plano on the Houston & Texas Central Railroad. Maybe the Rough Riders were still euphoric with their wins over Wylie because they were roughed up by their neighbors to the north. The Allen Wonders won the three-game series, two games to one.

During the summer of 1898, Ray's Rough Riders issued a challenge to the Texas Association's Fort Worth Panthers. For an independent team like Plano, beating a Texas Association team would be quite an accomplishment. Plano defeated Fort Worth in all three games. Next a challenge was sent south, to the Galveston Sand Crabs. The Galveston Sand Crabs were a dominant team in the last decade of the nineteenth century. They won the pennant in 1890; finished third in 1895; lost the league finals in 1896, finishing second; and won the pennant again in 1897. It would be a tall order for the Plano Nine to beat the mighty Sand Crabs.

Items representing the Plano Nine team on display at the Interurban Railway museum. *Interurban Railway Museum.*

All three games would be played in Galveston. So the Plano Nine met at the Plano Railroad Station and boarded a southbound Houston & Texas Central train. Game one began under the Gulf Coast sunshine but came to a halt due to darkness. After twelve hard-fought innings, the Sand Crabs and Rough Riders were tied at two runs apiece. Robert Howey, sportswriter for the *Plano Star-Courier*, wrote about the Rough Riders in a 1940 historical edition of the newspaper. He stated that after the 2–2 tie game, no other games were played between the Sand Crabs and Rough Riders because of the Spanish-American War.

History has buried the reason as to why the three-game series was cancelled so suddenly. Galveston was a member of the Texas Association in 1898 and it was a known fact that the league was struggling financially. Many players left the sport to serve in the Spanish-American War. Also the Galveston train depot was an arrival point for soldiers who had been training in San Antonio.

The Texas Association ceased operation mid-season due to the war. Fort Worth threw in the towel after 20 association games, Dallas after 21 games and San Antonio after 27. Galveston would be declared the second-half season champ with an overall record of 19-16, and the Austin Senators were declared winners of the first half of the season with an overall record of 18-12.

Ray's Rough Riders would have to settle for a tie with the powerful Galveston Sand Crabs.

DEATH ON THE RAIL

L ife changed dramatically for Plano when the railroad arrived in 1872. The railway brought more commerce to Plano—but it also brought crime and mayhem.

In those years, cotton was king. The trains linked Plano with McKinney and Dallas, turning Plano's downtown into the prosperous center of a booming farm economy. Thanks to the development of cheap fencing in the form of barbed wire and the introduction of mechanized farm equipment, cotton quickly became a very profitable crop. Visitors who look carefully can still spot pulleys and skylights in some of the buildings downtown where cotton bales were lifted into the buildings for inspection and trade.

A second railroad arrived in downtown Plano in 1908: the Texas Electric Railway, providing passenger service that linked Denison and Dallas by way of Plano.

There were several gruesome accidents involving the train, including a horrific story of a family who went out for a Sunday drive; their car was struck by a train, and two of the family members were killed instantly. Local newspapers carried accounts of the accident and injuries sustained, all in horrific detail.

Electricity also proved hazardous. If you're a fan of the TV show *Downton Abbey*, you may recall the scene where the Dowager Countess (Maggie Smith) refuses to turn on an electric light. In the early years, people were frightened by electricity, and in fact, it was dangerous because they didn't understand it. Maybe that's what led to the tragic end in 1909 of Larkin George, a young man in the employ of Philpott Hardware Company.

Above: In 1948, two Texas Electric interurban cars collided head-on at a curve near White Rock Creek. Forty-nine passengers were injured, but no one was killed. *Courtesy of the Johnnie J. Myers Research Center.*

Left: Another scene from the 1948 collision. *Courtesy of the Johnnie J. Myers Research Center.*

At about 8:30 p.m. on March 9, 1909, George was called in to work on connecting a pipe in the railway station, which is now home to the Interurban Railway Museum in downtown Plano. The station had only been open for about a year, and it's possible he didn't know much about electricity—how it worked or its dangers. George accidentally touched a high-tension wire up in the ceiling, still visible in the museum today, and was electrocuted. Physicians tried to resuscitate him, to no avail.

It was the second accident within the same year at the same station; another young man named Albert Blalock had also been burned there just a few months earlier. Blalock was cleaning the substation when he came in contact with a live wire carrying eighteen thousand volts. It burned the flesh off his right hand and arm. Blalock fell twenty feet to the cement floor and sustained a gash in the head, and his clothing caught fire. Luckily, a ticket agent was on duty and pulled him away from the wire and put out the fire.

Today, the DART Rail glides through downtown Plano at regular intervals, carrying residents to downtown Dallas and stops in between—for the most part, quietly and safely.

African American Entrepreneur in Jim Crow Texas

In 1910, one of Plano's first free African American residents arrived. A young man named Lee Andrew "L.A." Davis left his home in South Texas to find work as a sharecropper. Eventually, Davis would become a prominent leader in the Douglass Community, Plano's historically African American neighborhood.

At this time in history, African Americans dealt with strict segregation, harsh discrimination and virtually no economic opportunity. Under Jim Crow laws, black citizens were expected to eat at separate restaurants from white citizens, drink from separate water fountains, use separate restrooms and attend separate schools. Racial discrimination also made it very difficult to acquire property.

That didn't stop the entrepreneurial L.A. Davis. Ambitious and financially savvy, Davis became quite the businessman. Over time, he accumulated wealth through stocks and real estate.

Because of Davis's financial clout, he was able to purchase a large section of property in Plano's Douglass Community. He then sold plots of his property to local African Americans. In 1945, Davis also bought a plot of vacant land and established a burial site, the L.A. Davis Cemetery, reserved for African Americans from the Douglass Community.

Over time, the Davis Cemetery markers became overgrown with mold and moss, soiled from pollution and damaged by the severity and extremes of Texas weather. In 2015, the Plano Conservancy conducted its Tombstone Mysteries event at Davis Cemetery and the adjacent Old

Right: L.A. Davis. *Courtesy of Marcellus Davis.*

Below: Davis Cemetery plat. *Courtesy of Marcellus Davis.*

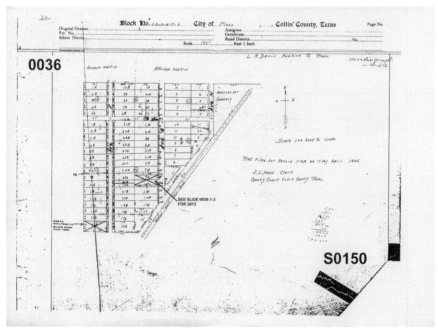

City Cemetery. Residents from the entire community came to learn how to clean gravestones and placed flowers on the graves of veterans. Tombstone Mysteries—a sort of scavenger hunt that sent visitors looking for interesting markers—allowed the participants to learn about the cemeteries' history. The event generated community awareness and appreciation for these two historic cemeteries.

Top: A view of the cemetery. *Photo by Jeff Campbell.*

Bottom: The grave of L.A. Davis. *Photo by Jeff Campbell.*

Land records and other mementos from L.A. Davis's life. *Plano Conservancy for Historic Preservation.*

In 2016, the Plano Conservancy for Historic Preservation received a grant from the City of Plano Heritage Commission to restore the cemetery. The first step was to install a new fence and gates around the two cemeteries. Next, working with Texas Cemetery Restoration, a plan of action was established. From October through December, the markers were cleaned, repaired and leveled. Next, a historic wayside sign was installed in Davis Cemetery to provide visitors with a brief history of the cemetery and its special importance to Plano's historic Douglass Community.

In January 2019, Preservation Texas awarded Jeff Campbell and the Plano Conservancy for Historic Preservation the Curtis Tunnell Award (Multicultural Heritage Project/Program) for the restoration work at Davis Cemetery. The cemetery that L.A. Davis established has become a historical treasure, a monument to citizens from Plano's past. The work undertaken at the cemetery ensures that it will remain a part of our city's rich cultural heritage for generations to come.

L.A. Davis came to Plano looking for opportunity. Not only did he make a good life for himself and others in his community, but he also left a legacy. Likely he never could have imagined Plano's incredible future or how his name would live on.

The Davis Cemetery is located in downtown Plano. The cemetery lies adjacent to the Old City Cemetery. From 15th Street, take H Avenue south. Both cemeteries are located on the left.

66

SILK HOSE TO BACKPACKS

While World War II raged thousands of miles away, the people back home in Plano found ways to do their part. In one unique recycling effort, the young ladies of the Thursday Study Club shifted their attention from books and loftier topics to help support the men and women in the Armed Forces.

In 1942, the club began to collect old rayon and silk hose to make into powder bags for the war, at the request of the Texas Federation of Women's Clubs. Club members were able to collect 114 pounds of stockings in just one month and sent them to the federation's headquarters in Austin. Other 1942 accomplishments included making 529 garments, hemming 143 diapers and knitting 400 to 500 sweaters and other articles. Club members also collected and sent 100 pounds of magazines to the War Veterans Hospital in Kerrville, Texas. Mrs. Van Stogner, chairman of the Conservation of National Resources, reported that forty tons of scrap metal, valued at $481, were collected during a drive, with the proceeds divided among various organizations of the town.

In February 1943, the National Red Cross encouraged Collin County and the women of Plano to turn their attention to organizing a surgical dressing room—a place to create surgical dressings from strips of cloth and package them to send overseas for use in treating injured soldiers. Because antibiotics were not widely used until the late 1940s, the dressings needed to be sterile to prevent infections. According to the club's minutes, Mrs. J.W. Britton said the

During World War II, worn silk stockings were collected throughout the country for conversion into powder bags used in naval defense weapons. *Franklin D. Roosevelt Library, public domain photograph.*

The Thursday Study Club held its regular by-monthly meeting on Nov 5, 1942 with Mrs. Henry Gist.

The course of study chosen by the Club for the year is South America, the first lesson being on Panama- Crossroads of the World. Mrs Frank Beverley talked on the Panama Canal and illustrated with objects, just how the locks work. Mrs. O. T. Mitchell spoke on The Conquest of the Tropics.

Mrs C. C. Aldredge, Chm. War Service, called for several reports from Standing Chairmen.

Mrs. Geo. Jones, Chm. Social & Industrial Relations, outlined plans for the silk stocking drive to be put on in Plano, for the purpose of making them into powder bags for defense.

Mrs. J. W. Britton, chm, Red Cross. reported 52 garments had been made by Red Cross workers during the past 2 weeks. Mrs. Huguley, Chm. Knitting, reported 400 garments made by Plano ladies this year.

Mrs. J. F. Harrington, who was on

Thursday Study Club minutes, November 5, 1942. *Plano Public Library, Plano, Texas.*

The Thursday Study Club met on nov. 19 with Mrs. J. W. Britton. The membership was 100% in attendance.

Mrs. T. L. Batchelor brought a map & geography study of South America & Mrs. Van Stoenen gave some outstanding developments in the history of South America.

Mrs. Geo. W. Jones reported 114 lbs. of silk stockings had been forwarded to Headquarters—Austin to be used in the making of gun powder bags. The collection of old hose is to continue for the duration.

Mrs. S. Y. Carpenter, Chm, War Bonds & Stamps, announced that from nov 22-28, would be "Women at War Week," & asked that we co-operate with our city chm.

Mrs. J. F. Harrington, presented Mrs. Fay Thomas' name for membership

Mrs. Fortner moved that we dispense with the rules & vote today in order for her to come into the club the next meeting—Carried.

Mrs. Thomas was unanimously

Thursday Study Club minutes, November 19, 1942. *Plano Public Library, Plano, Texas.*

immee to give reports:—

Mrs. Arthur Baguell, Chm, Bible, made an interesting talk + led in prayer.

Mrs. Britton, chm. Red Cross, reported 529 garments made, 143 diapers hemmed + between 4 + 500 sweaters + articles knitted during 1942.

Mrs. Geo. Jones, chm. Social + Industrial Relations, reported on hosiery drive + urged that the ladies continue to save their discarded ~~silk~~ + nilons.

Mrs. Carpenter, talked on stamps + bonds.

Mrs. J.F. Harrington, Chm. Legislation, asked that we as club women, write to our Representatives in Austin, requesting them to seek additional federal aid for our schools, due to reduction in gasoline tax.

Mrs. Stogner, Chm. Conservation of National Resources, reported having personally sent about 100 lbs. magazines to the War Veteran's Hospital, at Kerrville, Tex.

Mrs. Batchelor reported on Junior Club, due to the absence of the Councilor, Mrs. Skaggs.

Thursday Study Club minutes, January 7, 1943. *Plano Public Library, Plano, Texas.*

American Legion Home had a room secured for the Surgical Dressing Room Unit for Plano. Mayor Schell and others had the room thoroughly cleaned and made ready. Mrs. Si Harrington became the chairman of the Surgical Dressing Room Unit, and everyone was urged to help. Also in 1943, the group collected twenty books to send to the young men in the Armed Forces.

From October 1944 to April 1945, the group temporarily disbanded so that members could help the Red Cross and serve as aides in the hospital.

ABOUT THE THURSDAY STUDY CLUB

By the time the war broke out, the Thursday Study Club had been meeting for almost three decades. The club began in 1914, when a group of young women, realizing the need for intellectual growth and aesthetic development, met in the home of Miss Vivian Gulledge. These educated young ladies wanted to keep informed and to learn something new every day.

The charter members of Plano's first literary club included Miss Gulledge, the first president; Mrs. James Adams, Miss Frances Aldridge, Mrs. E.C. Allen, Mrs. J.W. Britton, Miss Idalee Carlisle, Miss Maud Davis, Mrs. Ray Jasper, Miss Geraldine Schimelpfenig, Mrs. C.J. Matthews, Mrs. Louis Pellering, Mrs. Dave Reed, Mrs. J.D. Newsome, Miss Effie Skinner and Miss Edna Russell. Many other women from well-known Plano families served as president over the years. The membership was limited to twenty, and there was always a long waiting list to join.

Club members also organized the Junior Thursday Study Club for their daughters and their friends in high school. Both clubs were part of the Texas Federation of Women's Clubs.

Among topics they studied over the years were the American home and family; music, art and literature; our American heritage; "What is Americanism?"; community and civic affairs; crime and safety measures; and many more. They also tackled special projects, including cleaning and replanting Old Plano Cemetery; contributing $100 to Haggard Park; donating $100 to the Public Library; providing food baskets and toys for the needy at Thanksgiving and Christmas; and many other very valuable projects.

Club members held the final meeting on May 9, 2002, and contributed their minutes, yearbooks and other materials to the Genealogy Center of the Plano Public Library. The items are available to view online at the Plano Public Library's Collin County Images website.

PLANO'S IRON LUNG

Just as the United States was finally leaving the nightmare of World War II behind, another tragedy loomed on the horizon: the polio epidemic. As in other times in Plano's history, citizens rallied together to face the challenge.

In its worst year, 1952, nearly 58,000 cases of polio were reported in the United States, with 3,145 dead and 21,269 left with mild to disabling paralysis. The viral disease struck fear in the hearts of communities. Parents kept their children at home and away from crowded places.

To ensure that children who contracted polio could receive lifesaving emergency treatment as they were transported to the hospital, Plano citizens pooled their funds in 1947 and equipped the volunteer fire department with an iron lung. It took just hours to raise the money needed: $1,209, or about $13,000 in today's dollars.

This inspiring—but hidden—story was uncovered in 2018 when the Genealogy Center of the Plano Public Library embarked on a project transcribing the surviving minutes and ledgers from Plano's Volunteer Fire Department, ranging from about 1904 to the 1970s.

According to those minutes, on February 4, 1947, W.T. Nickerson of Dallas "gave a very interesting and instructive demonstration with an iron lung" to the Plano Fire Department. Two weeks later, the department met in a special called meeting to form a committee to solicit funds from the merchants of Plano to purchase the device. After some discussion, Fire Chief Standifer appointed Homer Horton as chairman, with E.J. Baxter, R.B. Howey and Dr. O.T. Mitchell named to assist in the effort.

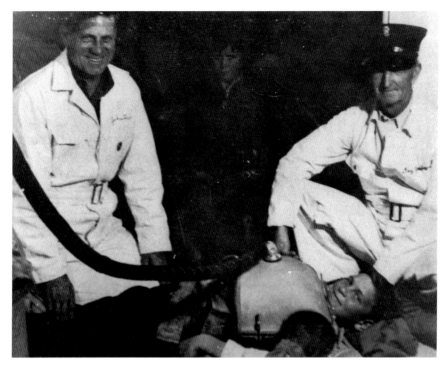

Firemen showing young people how the iron lung works. *Plano Public Library, Plano, Texas.*

On March 4, Horton reported the good news: all of the money needed to purchase the iron lung—$1,209—had been raised in only six hours. A list of the names of donors and the amount each had given was entered into the minutes, including the Rotary Club ($100); Dr. O.T. Mitchell ($50); the City of Plano ($100); Harrington Funeral Home ($100); First National Bank ($10); the Chamber of Commerce ($100); and Charley Christie ($50). The meeting minutes also noted that the department was drilled on the operation of the iron lung, with each member taking part.

The iron lung was the only hope for saving polio victims in respiratory distress. Polio, or poliomyelitis, is a viral disease that causes paralysis. In the acute, early stages, many patients are unable to breathe as the virus paralyzes muscles in the chest. Many died in this stage, but those who survived usually recovered much or almost all of their former strength.

No effective means to help keep victims breathing during that acute phase was available until 1927, when Philip Drinker and Louis Agassiz Shaw at Harvard University devised a version of a tank respirator that could maintain respiration artificially until a person could breathe

114

Donations for Iron Lung.

Alex Schell	$10.00	C. E. Hood	$5.00
Rotary Club	$100.00	Raymond Hinton	$5.00
Dr. O. F. Mitchell	$50.00	E. A. Sigler	$10.00
Bill Bishop	$25.00	J. W. Shapp	$5.00
Jack Harris Bro	$25.00	Tyrell Carpenter	$25.00
Joe Bradshaw	$10.00	Plano Consum Co-op	$25.00
A. L. Merritt	$5.00	Owens Grain Co	$25.00
Mrs. Alma Perry	$2.00	Home Ice Co	$10.00
E. F. Griffin Man Store	$20.00	R. M. Swindle	$5.00
Geo W. Jones	$5.00	J. A. Swindle	$5.00
J. D. Oneal	$5.00	Roy Jones	$5.00
W. T. Griffin	$1.00	Miller Dress Shop	$8.00
Brady Smith	$10.00	J. F. Howell	$1.50
Joe Griffin	$10.00	Roy Lewis	$2.00
Harry Steenson	$5.00	Edd Haun	$1.00
City of Plano	$100.00	W. L. Haun	$1.00
Speedy Anderson	$10.00	C. F. Baxter	$10.00
D. L. Garrison	$2.50	Palace Theater	$20.00
Harrington T. Home	$100.00	J. D. Reed	$2.00
A. H. Johnson	$1.00	Sam Stillwel	$1.00
Moore Variety Store	$2.50	Plano School	$100.00
Ray Hendrix	$1.00		
J. A. Maultsby	$1.00		
A. Weatherford	$10.00		
F. J. Vanira	$10.00		
H. T. Miller	$2.00	The Total amount of
Harrington phy	$25.00	Donation was 1228
C. P. Harrington	$10.00	for the Purchas of the Iron Lung
Earl Wetsel	$10.00	The Iron Lung cost 1209.00
Dr. J. R. Thompson	$25.00	Leaving out Bal ance of $19.50 over
Lester Floyd	$10.00	Subscribed
A. A. Bagwill	$25.00	
James Harrington	$10.00	
First Nat. Bank	$400.00	
Fred Harrington	$5.00	
Co-op Gro & Mkt	$25.00	
Chamber of Com.	$100.00	
Charley Christie	$50.00	
Dr. S. D. Wyatt	$50.00	
Hinton Gro Mkt	$25.00	
J. W. Robinson	$2.00	
Ralph Thorp	$10.00	
James Hays	$10.00	
John Brodhead	$5.00	
Strange & Coaths	$10.00	
D. F. Wilson	$5.00	approved - 4-1-19-47
Sec Trea Bill Smith		Chief Standefy

Donations from the citizens of Plano to purchase the iron lung for the Plano Volunteer Fire Department. *Plano Fire-Rescue/Plano Public Library, Plano, Texas.*

independently, usually after one or two weeks. The machine was powered by an electric motor with two vacuum cleaners. The pump changed the pressure inside a rectangular, airtight metal box, pulling air in and out of the lungs. Inventor John Emerson later refined the device and cut the cost nearly in half. Inside the tank respirator, the patient lay on a bed (sometimes called a "cookie tray") that could slide in and out of the cylinder as needed. The side of the tank had portal windows so attendants could reach in and adjust limbs, sheets or hot packs.

From the 1930s to the 1950s, the iron lung saved thousands of people, mostly children, from otherwise certain death. The Plano Fire Department's ledger mentions at least one potentially lifesaving use of the device in Plano. The iron lung was taken to Paul Junker's farm on May 25, 1948.

Other mentions of the iron lung crop up in the minutes until 1953, including frequent drills on the proper use of the device. At one of the practice sessions, local Boy Scouts attended and learned about the iron lung.

ABOUT PLANO'S FIRE DEPARTMENT

Today, Plano Fire-Rescue is the tenth-largest fire department in the state of Texas, providing fire protection and emergency medical services to the city's more than 286,000 residents. This proud organization traces its beginnings to 1887.

Plano's Eclipse Fire Company, the city's first fire department, was organized as a bucket brigade led by Chief J.A. Moreman and fought many fires in Plano. To supply water for the bucket brigades, a dedicated well was dug at the intersection of Main and Mechanic Streets (now K Avenue and 15th).

City council soon realized the city needed more equipment and ordered a chemical engine in 1893 and, the following year, built a city hall with a calaboose (jail) and place for the fire apparatus.

In March 1894, the city council elected six men for the Plano Fire Department: A.G. Stopple, R.C. Hays, Clint Mathews, John Morgan, Stewart Kendrick and John Gates as chief. In 1897, an alarm bell was installed atop city hall to alert the "Fire Boys" when a fire broke out. Over the years, city council reorganized the fire department several times, and by 1904, the city council had hired Murry "Dag" Hudson to serve as Plano's first professional firefighter.

In 1915, the fire department modernized from horse-drawn vehicles to motorized equipment. A Thomas Flyer automobile was converted by the firemen, with help from local mechanics, at a cost of $350. By 1917, a second Thomas Flyer was converted into a combination hose and ladder with a chemical tank, ending the era of the horse-drawn fire engines. The first pumper was named "Big Tom" and served from 1915 to 1929. The next pumper, by Peter-Pirsch & Sons, was purchased for $7,500. By 1930, the fire department had increased to twenty-one members.

Over the years, the fire department hosted many fundraisers to help pay for equipment, uniforms and other supplies. These events included plays, suppers and even a circus. The City of Plano purchased several different fire trucks as needed, and in 1961, the Lone Star Boat Company even donated a boat for water rescues.

The fire department continued to add men and equipment to keep up with the growth of Plano. In 1963, the department had four paid firemen and twenty-two volunteer firemen. In 1949, the City of Plano had 55 fire plugs; by 1963, 188 plugs were in place. The Central Fire Station was built and dedicated in 1966, replacing the two-story brick building that had served as the first station since 1923.

Editor's note: Librarians hope to discover more great stories from the Plano Fire Department as they continue the transcription of the department's meeting minutes. More photographs and documents will be added on an ongoing basis. Check the Collin County Images, Plano Fire Department Collection, at glhtadigital.contentdm.oclc.org/digital/collection/ p15915coll21 for more "hidden history" of Plano's great fire department. Or visit the Genealogy Center at the Haggard Library in Plano to learn more.

Plano's Fire Bell

This fire bell was purchased for $57.50 when the Plano Fire Department was formed in 1897 and was used to call volunteer firefighters to a fire. Before the department purchased the bell, volunteers were summoned with three pistol shots fired in rapid succession.

The bell was purchased from Belknap Hardware Company in Kentucky and was manufactured by the C.S. Bell Company. The double bell clapper increased resonance and response time. It was phased out in 1934 when a five-horsepower siren was placed at city hall.

Bell in front of Fire Station No. 1 today. *Plano Fire-Rescue/Plano Public Library, Plano, Texas.*

Left: Bell (*top left on roof*) of the fire station in 1906. *Plano Fire-Rescue/Plano Public Library, Plano, Texas.*

Below: Bell in front of Fire Station No. 1 with honor guard. *Plano Fire-Rescue.*

Today, Plano residents can see the bell in front of Plano Fire Department Station 1 on K Avenue. The plaque with the bell reads: "May it serve future generations as a reminder of the proud traditions of community service by the Plano Fire Department."[20]

SWIM FROM EL PASO TO TEXARKANA

D id you know that you can swim from Texarkana to El Paso—all without leaving Plano? Dive into one of Plano's most interesting landmarks, the Texas Pool, and swim any way you like across the great state of Texas.

Believed to be the oldest Texas-shaped pool in existence, the Texas Pool recently earned a designation from the National Register of Historic Places. It's located on Plano's east side at 901 Springbrook Drive and was built as part of one of Plano's earliest large residential developments, called Dallas North Estates, by one of Texas's most iconic families.

Touted as a "Texas size and Texas-shaped swimming pool for residents," the Texas Pool opened to the public on Memorial Day 1961 to much fanfare. Residents were invited to guess the capacity of the saltwater concrete pool (168,000 gallons), with the best guess winning a boat, a trailer and a motor from the Lone Star Boat Company in Plano. The 1962 Miss Plano beauty contest was held at the Texas Pool that first summer, sponsored by the Plano Chamber of Commerce, with seventeen women competing and a young lady named Shirley Renfrow capturing the crown. Quickly, the pool became the summer hangout spot of choice for Plano children and teens.

Aerial view of the Texas Pool. *City of Plano.*

SUMMER MEMORIES

Every time she hears "Hooked on a Feeling" or "Brandy" on the radio, Mabrie Griffith Jackson remembers moon pies, cute bikinis and the smell of chlorine at the Texas Pool. As with many longtime Plano residents, the pool was the scene of many fond memories.

"I spent every summer there for nine years," she said. "We would ride our bikes to a creek and cross over a tree that had fallen (praying we wouldn't lose our balance) to get to the pool."

The Texas Pool was also the place where Jackson took her first try at the high dive, and "I nearly drowned," she recalled.

Many multigenerational memories were made at the Texas Pool. One woman served as a lifeguard in the 1970s, and her daughter later did the same. Officer David Tilley of the Plano Police Department remembers his father serving on the pool's board of directors. His parents moved to North Dallas Estates in 1961; Officer Tilley was born a year later, in 1962. "I was going to the pool from the time I was a toddler all the way up until probably until age seventeen," Officer Tilley said.

He remembers an island in the pool, located at roughly the spot where Plano would fall on the map of Texas, with a big slide. Kids would jump off the high dive in a deliberate attempt to splash the lifeguard. Create a big enough splash and the lifeguard would kick you out of the pool for a while—a badge of honor among the kids. "I guess that would be my first experience of violating the rules," he said with a chuckle.

Officer Tilley also remembers how his mother would allow him, as a preteen, to ride his bike to the pool and stay there for hours—by himself. "It's a different world back in the '60s and '70s," he said. "Everybody knew each other. My parents trusted the lifeguards to keep an eye on us."

It was a different world, indeed, which points to one sad bit of historical context in this story. During the time the pool was built, African American Texans were protesting segregation by staging sit-ins at diners and stores in Dallas. While segregation was banned at some public facilities, many pools remained off-limits to African Americans. Between 1950 and 1970, many Americans chose to stop swimming in municipal pools due to civil rights conflicts. While there may not have been a policy of segregation at the Texas Pool, given the timing, the "amenity" of a racially exclusive swimming pool may have appealed to at least some of Plano's primarily white residents in the 1960s.

BUILT BY TEXANS

The pool is not just shaped like Texas; it was built by one of Texas's most famous and colorful families. Herbert Hunt and Hunt Properties were the developers of Dallas North Estates. Herbert's father was oil and gas tycoon H.L. Hunt, a larger-than-life figure who had amassed $600 million by 1948 (equivalent to more than $6 billion in today's dollars). H.L. had fifteen children, several of whom carried on the family's business legacy. (Another child of H.L.'s whose name you may recognize: Margaret Hunt Hill, namesake of the iconic bridge in Dallas.)

Hunt Properties developed Dallas North Estates, some 1,700 acres of homes, schools, churches and parks that "started from a Plano wheat field," according to the *Dallas Morning News*. The neighborhood consisted of three- to five-bedroom homes priced between $10,700 and $15,000. Herbert Hunt chose the name "Dallas North Estates" because, he later said, "nobody would know where in the heck Plano was." The builder was George Chapman of Chapman Homes, who had just finished a 3,000-home development, Casa View, in Dallas near White Rock Lake. The final plat for Dallas North Estates was approved in September 1960, and work began at once. By October, all 153 lots had been sold. When the first model homes opened in March 1961,

Herbert Hunt, the
developer of North
Dallas Estates, in 2009.
Courtesy the Texas Pool.

home shoppers who visited the models were offered a free pass to the pool
for the month of June.

North Dallas Estates was the pioneer that led the building boom that
turned Plano from a sleepy farming town into a burgeoning suburb
beginning in the 1960s. In a 1962 article in the *Plano Daily-Star Courier*,
a representative of Hunt Enterprises shared his vision of continued
development that would "accommodate a population of 100,000 in the
Plano area in the years to come."

SAVED FROM DESTRUCTION

The swimming spot remained popular well into the 1990s, with long
lines of families camping out every spring to sign up for an annual
membership. But by 2007, the Texas Pool was in danger of being lost.
The neighborhood had aged. The children of the original families who
bought homes there in the 1960s and 1970s had grown up and moved
away. More women went to work, and children were no longer at home
in the summer with nothing else to do but hang out at the pool. On top
of all that, the economy was sluggish, and annual fees were costly—
about $350 per year. Membership dwindled to about fifty families—too
few to cover the maintenance costs of the pool. By 2007, the association
of residents who oversaw the pool was poised to close the pool and hand
the property over to the city.

Then resident Janet Vermillion Moos stepped in.

"'Impossible' and 'No' are not words I understand very well," Janet said.

Moos organized residents to save the pool. They changed its structure, from a private club exclusive to residents of the development to a communitywide gathering place.

"We were saving the pool one season at a time," said Moos.

In 2010, the group began to look for ways to preserve the pool indefinitely. In 2013, they created a nonprofit 501(c)(3), the Texas Pool Foundation, and began the process of turning the spot into a historic landmark. Moos serves as founder and CEO. The old board dissolved and merged in 2016, with one board and one vision for the Texas Pool.

By 2018, the pool was back in business, with a membership of 225 families. It's a big, community-wide effort. Families can barter services to join instead of paying fees; the maintenance, management and marketing for the pool are all done by volunteers. Currently, the only paid staff are the lifeguards.

Front entrance to the Texas Pool, 2019. *Courtesy of the Texas Pool.*

HIDDEN CITIES

Following an exhaustive application process, the Texas Pool was listed in the National Register of Historic Places on April 1, 2019, as the first and oldest Texas-shaped pool in the world.

And one of the pool's favorite features was recently restored. As part of a renovation effort in 2018, a building crew discovered the original tiles under a vinyl floor covering that marked the locations of major Texas cities on the bottom of the pool.

"The original tiles were covered over at some point in the 1970s," Moos said. "We have a deficit of history from the mid-'70s to the mid-'80s. There wasn't any documentation, and we don't have any photographs, so we don't have many pictures of how it looked back then. All we know is that, at some point, the bottom was covered over and the tiles were lost."

Thanks to a grant from the City of Plano's Heritage Commission, the Texas Pool commissioned artist Tony Holman to re-create the original seven city tiles at his Plano pottery studio, as well as four new tiles. So when the pool opened in May 2019, once again, residents were once again able to swim from Texarkana to El Paso—without leaving Plano.

Pagoda on the Prairie

Driving across the Texas plains in the late 1960s, you'd expect to see new subdivisions or fields with barbed wire and pastures. But a pagoda? Probably not.

Yet Plano did indeed have its very own pagoda, and it was not a Chinese restaurant or a martial arts studio. The pagoda was the centerpiece of the University of Plano, one of the strangest stories in Plano's hidden history.

The University of Plano was the creation of Robert J. Morris, a native of New Jersey who moved to Texas in 1960. Over the years, Texans would come to view Morris as either passionate, crazy, conniving—or all three.

"Anybody who puts up a pagoda in Plano has got to be suspect," wrote John Merwin in a 1975 *D Magazine* article titled "The Strange Case of Plano University."[21]

Morris was a nationally known conservative firebrand who railed, along with Joe McCarthy, against communism. Twice he served as counsel on the Senate Judiciary Subcommittee on Internal Security, from 1951 to 1953 and again from 1956 to 1958. After failing to win a 1958 U.S. Senate race in his native New Jersey, Morris moved to Texas in 1960 and became president of the University of Dallas. His term would last only two years. His university colleagues were shocked by his incessant political anti-communism rants. His outspokenness led to his forced resignation in 1962. During his years in Texas, he ran for U.S. Senate twice, started an ultraconservative group called the Defenders of American Liberties and founded a university.

Dr. Robert Morris. *Plano Public Library, Plano, Texas.*

Morris ran for U.S. Senate twice, in 1964 and 1970. In both races, he lost the Republican primary to future president George Herbert Walker Bush. The 1964 campaign made him an enemy of the Texas Republican Party, and he came in third in the primary. When he tried again to beat Bush in the 1970 Republican primary, he lost handily, 87 percent to 12 percent.

"I knew I didn't stand a chance in '68," Morris told *D Magazine* in 1975. "But sometimes you run for office to get a forum to say things that need to be said." It's worth noting that Bush went on to lose both general elections, to Democratic incumbent Ralph W. Yarborough in 1964 and to Lloyd M. Bentsen Jr., also a Democrat, in 1970.

After leaving the University of Dallas, Morris organized the Defenders of American Liberties, closely modeled after the American Civil Liberties Union but with a very different political agenda. The group's first cause was to defend former major general Edwin A. Walker, who was accused of inciting unrest on the campus of the University of Mississippi when James Meredith tried to enroll as the school's first black student.

However, Morris unveiled his most outlandish pursuit in 1964: the launch of the University of Plano. Originally known as the University of Lebanon, the name was changed to reflect the new campus to be constructed in Plano, Texas. The campus would be located on Custer Road between Park Boulevard and Parker Road.

Persuasive by nature, Morris was able to get the Malaysian government to donate a twelve-thousand-square-foot pagoda to the effort. This building would become the infamous centerpiece of the university, housing the school's administration offices and library. The pagoda had originally served as the government of Malaysia's pavilion at the 1964 World's Fair in New York. A dedication was held on April 6, 1966, with Plano mayor R.L. Harrington and a delegation from the Malaysian government in attendance.

Morris's motivation for building the school was his son's disabilities. Willie Morris did not speak until he was three years old and was described as having a "fuzzy look" in his eyes.[22] Most likely Willie was slightly autistic, but given the limited knowledge at the time, he was diagnosed as having sustained brain damage at birth. Through therapy, Willie was able to attend regular kindergarten; meanwhile, Morris became obsessed with the idea that there must be numerous children with slight learning disabilities who could not attend college.

In the beginning, the university implemented techniques from the Doman-Delacato Method, which emphasized crawling and creeping as a way of stimulating brain development. Through the years, the American Academy of Pediatrics has voiced warnings about these methods. As late as 2010, the academy reaffirmed its views, stating, "This treatment is based on an outmoded and oversimplified theory of brain development. Current information does not support the claims of proponents that this treatment is efficacious, and its use continues to be unwarranted....The demands and expectations placed on families are so great that in some cases their financial resources may be depleted substantially and parental and sibling relationships could be stressed."[23]

The University of Plano continued offering special needs programs and a liberal arts curriculum through the 1960s and early 1970s, at one time even fielding a baseball team. The team's moment in the sun was losing four games of a four-game series to the 1975 National Champion Texas Longhorns by a combined score of 26–1.

Most universities in the United States have endowments, usually amassed through donations. The University of Plano had very little in donations;

University of Plano with the pagoda, imported from Malaysia, in the background. *Plano Public Library, Plano, Texas.*

instead, the institution's endowment was based on land speculation. As the corridor along Highway 75 began to prosper, Morris started buying and selling land to support the school's endowment.

Merwin quoted a Housing and Urban Development (HUD) official whom he contacted to ask about land financing in Plano. "Oh yes, I've heard about that guy [Morris]," he said. "I've heard he takes his half off the real estate sales first and then leaves the school what's left."

In 1967, the new university was in danger of losing accreditation, and by the 1970s, the university was losing more than $400,000 a year. Morris was also losing his reputation with the local community as he continued trying to hustle real estate.

Morris never developed a good relationship with the Plano City Council and failed to convince the council to approve his request to have his land zoned commercial so that he could sell it at a higher price.

The 1975 *D Magazine* article was unsparing in its assessment. "Word has it that the University of Plano is nothing but a front for a real estate gambit for some pseudo-academic rip-off artist who claims he's running a university but in fact is buying and selling 'university land' all over North America and pocketing the profits," Merwin wrote in the *D Magazine* story. "You might have heard it is some kind of a right-wing indoctrination center—a place where a crazy old man locks students in the library and won't let them out until they're ready to fight the conspiracy."

Soon, the scheme fell apart. As Plano developed, the opportunities to buy and sell land diminished. Morris started to sell off the campus property. The seven-hundred-acre university campus would shrink to thirty acres by the mid-1970s. Then Morris began to look globally for land acquisition.

But Morris didn't stop dreaming. There were plans for a campus in Washington, D.C., and one on the Baja of Mexico, neither of which ever materialized. Also, a loan was taken out to buy over one thousand acres near the Garza–Little Elm Reservoir for an environmental science program that never came about. The loan for this land was strangling the university to death.

Morris even scheduled a baseball game with the University of Notre Dame. The game would be played in Plano on the university's foreclosed football field. The idea was that the game would raise money and help publicize the university. But like Morris's other ideas, this one never came to fruition either.

The school would continue to lose money and fight lawsuits, and finally a recession wiped out the University of Plano in 1976. With an enrollment of two hundred to three hundred students, and many of those from out of town, there aren't many local alumni to carry on the memory of Plano University.

Morris returned to New Jersey, taking the school's transcripts with him, and continued to write. He ran one more failed U.S. Senate campaign and finally, in 1996, died of heart failure at the age of eighty-two.

The authors wish to thank D Magazine *and the* Plano Star Courier *for their research.*

PLANO'S OWN MILITARY TANK

Next to the playground in Liberty Park in Plano, you'll find a military tank. It's an M41A3 Walker Bulldog tank, weighing in at 23.5 tons, built in 1953 and used in the Korean and Vietnam Wars. The tank had a top speed of forty-five miles per hour, a range of one hundred miles and, when fully armed, came equipped with a 76mm cannon and a .50-caliber machine gun on top.

So, what's a tank doing on a playground in Plano?

The tank was originally acquired from the Redstone Arsenal by Dr. Tom Allen, who was then curating a history museum envisioned for the campus of the University of Plano. Plans for the museum were abandoned a few years later, but the tank remained on the campus, then located between Park Boulevard and Parker Road off Custer.

At one point, Plano kids were able to get inside the tank, sit in the driver's seat and spin the turret. (It has since been welded shut, in the interest of safety.)

Longtime Plano residents remember the tank on the campus and later in front of the Dairy Queen on 14th Street. On at least one occasion, the tank rolled through downtown Plano for the holiday parade. One resident recalls the time when the tank was moved to Liberty Park—by air! A helicopter picked it up and relocated the tank.

Richard Grady, a Plano city councilman, knows the tank well from firsthand experience—but not in Plano. He's a Vietnam veteran.

"It was designed as a reconnaissance tank and replaced the M24 Chaffee," he said. "It's named after General Walton 'Johnny' Walker and was later

The tank in Liberty Park is a remnant of the University of Plano. *Photo by Mary Jacobs.*

replaced by the M551 Sheridan. You had to open the turret door and stand halfway out of the tank to use the gun, which put you in a vulnerable position. The advantage was you had about a 270-degree field of fire, versus the 45-degree field of fire with the front-mounted .30-caliber gun. If you hit someone with a .50-caliber round, they were not getting back up."

STEINDAM'S SACRIFICE IN VIETNAM

On February 1, 1970, darkness fell in Tây Ninh Province, close to the Cambodian border in Vietnam. Army first lieutenant Russell Steindam prepared to lead his platoon on an ambush operation. The Vietnam War would rage on for five more years, but for Steindam, his war would end on that dark, crimson night.

Russell Albert Steindam was born on August 27, 1946, in Austin, Texas. His family moved to Plano when he was five years old. An exceptional student, Russell was one of the few Plano High School ninth graders to receive a National Development Test Award in 1961. He graduated in 1964 as a National Honor Society member. Sandra Braden Coleman, who attended school with Steindam, remembers him as an industrious young man who worked with other schoolmates on a ranch off Preston Road.

Not only was Russell an excellent student and hard worker, but he also displayed the skills of encouragement and motivation at a young age. Margaret Ruth Erwin Stephens shared the following story. "Russell was my brother-in-law. One of my first memories of him was when he and my sister asked me to join them to go to a play at the Dallas Music Hall. That was a big deal for me, and I was so excited. I was a shy, awkward young girl with not much self-confidence. When Russell held the door for me to leave the house, he looked at me and said, 'You look pretty, Margaret. Soon you will be a beautiful young woman.' I will never forget how good that made me feel. That was just Russell. He was such an awesome guy and always tried to make people around him feel good."

PROPHETS
Sue Nevels
Russell Steindam

Russell Steindam (*left*) was named "Class Prophet" at Plano Senior High. *Plano Public Library, Plano, Texas.*

After leaving Plano High School, Steindam returned to Austin and enrolled at the University of Texas, joining the ROTC. He received a two-year Army Reserve Officer Training Corps Scholarship that paid for tuition, textbooks, laboratory fees and a fifty-dollar-per-month subsistence allowance.

After earning his bachelor's degree in 1968, he joined the United States Army and arrived in South Vietnam on October 1, 1969, leaving his pregnant wife, Mary, back in Texas. Steindam excelled as an Army Ranger and an armored vehicle commander.

As he led his men on that fateful February night, the darkness exploded in sound and fury. Steindam and his platoon came under a fierce Viet Cong fusillade of automatic weapons, small arms fire and rocket-launched and hand grenades.

Steindam, out in the open and exposed to peril, ordered his troops to return fire. Then he directed the efforts to move the wounded soldiers to the cover of a bomb crater. Suddenly, a fragmentation grenade was hurled into his area. In the blink of an eye, Steindam shouted a warning to his platoon while flinging his body on the grenade. Steindam took the full force of the explosion, sacrificing his life to save the lives of his comrades.

Steindam's unparalleled act of valor and bravery resulted not only in a Purple Heart but also the Medal of Honor and two Bronze Stars. Steindam's remains were buried in Dallas at Restland Park. "He was an interesting young man who loved his country and his family. He never saw his son. What a loss for us," Sandra Coleman said.

Throughout the years, Steindam's act of sacrifice and bravery has not been forgotten. In 1972, the University of Texas ROTC building was named Russell A. Steindam Hall. In 1993, the City of Plano named Lieutenant Russell Steindam Park in his honor.

In November 2017, the Collin County Commissioners Court, in a unanimous 5–0 vote, chose to rename the county courthouse the Russell A. Steindam Courts Building—a fitting memorial to a selfless hometown hero.

A NATIVE AMERICAN IN SPACE

When he was a boy, John Herrington watched the moon landing on TV and dreamed of space exploration. He even built his own spaceship out of a cardboard box. "I was dreaming about being an astronaut, but not realizing it was something I could actually accomplish," he said in a recent interview. "Thirty years later, I'm not in a cardboard box. I'm 40 years old and I'm sitting in the real thing."[24]

The "real thing" was STS-113 *Endeavour*, the sixteenth shuttle mission to visit the International Space Station, in 2002. With that mission, the 1976 Plano Senior High alum became the first Native American in space.

"It was an amazing experience," he said.

Herrington was born on September 14, 1958, in Wetumka, Oklahoma, in the Chickasaw Nation. He grew up in Colorado Springs, Colorado; Riverton, Wyoming; and Plano, Texas. He played the saxophone in the band at Plano Senior High School and graduated in 1976.

For college, Herrington returned to Colorado, to the mountains he'd loved as a child, with plans to become a forest ranger. "I didn't know what a forest ranger did, except they work outside," he told *McCall Digest* in 2018.[25]

He spent more time rock climbing than studying. With a 1.72 grade point average, he was kicked out of school after the second semester. Then he went to work on a road crew, earning four dollars an hour rappelling along canyon walls to make measurements needed to build Interstate 70.

"Fate had more in mind for Herrington than just a cool job hanging from cliffs, for this is when and how the college dropout discovered his true calling," according to *McCall Digest*. Herrington became curious and asked how the team performed calculations from the measurements he was collecting. A light bulb went off.

"What I had seen in a textbook was now, 'Oh, that's how it works,'" he said. "Math suddenly not only made sense, but was cool, and fun. And guys got paid to do it."

He returned to college with new energy. "They [the college] actually let me back in, which was amazing," Herrington said. "Now I understood the purpose behind the math. I had a great instructor who I took all my math from, college algebra and trig—didn't take trig in high school—all my calculus."

A faculty member asked Herrington to tutor a retired navy captain who was pursuing a degree and needed help with calculus. Herrington agreed. Here's how *McCall Digest* describes the encounter:

> *"This guy flew dive bombers in WWII and was one of the first hundred helicopter pilots in the US Navy," Herrington says, remembering how impressed he was at the time. As often happens, the older man asked the college kid what he wanted to be when he grew up. "He said, 'You should join the Navy and do what I did,'" Herrington recalls. "He explained what he did, and it sounded so exciting. He said, 'Go see the movie* Officer and a Gentleman; *that's what you'll have to do.' As a college graduate, to join the Navy you have to go to Officer Candidate's School. To be a Naval Aviator during the 1980's you had to go to Aviation Officer Candidate School in Pensacola, Florida. I went and saw the movie, and thought, yeah, that looks exciting. So I took the test—things like spatial awareness and mechanical aptitude—and I did well."*

After earning his bachelor's degree in applied mathematics from the University of Colorado–Colorado Springs, Herrington received his commission in the United States Navy in 1984. He was designated a naval aviator and proceeded to Patrol Squadron Thirty-One (VP-31) at Moffett Field, California, for training in the P-3C Orion. His first operational assignment was with Patrol Squadron Forty-Eight (VP-48) where he made three operational deployments, two to the Northern Pacific–based Naval Air Facility Adak in Alaska and one to the Western Pacific–based Naval Air Station Cubi Point in the Philippines. While assigned to VP-48, Herrington was designated a patrol plane commander, mission commander and patrol plane instructor pilot.[26]

Following completion of his first operational tour, Herrington returned to VP-31 as a fleet replacement squadron instructor pilot. While assigned to VP-31, he was selected to attend the United States Naval Test Pilot School at Naval Air Station Patuxent River, Maryland, in January 1990. After graduation in 1990, he reported to the Force Warfare Aircraft Test Directorate as a project test pilot for the Joint Primary Aircraft Training System. Herrington conducted additional flight test assignments flying numerous variants of the P-3 Orion as well as the T-34C and the de Havilland Canada Dash 7. Following his selection as an aeronautical engineering duty officer (AEDO), Herrington reported to the U.S. Naval Postgraduate School, where he attained a master of science degree in aeronautical engineering in June 1995. Herrington was assigned as a special projects officer to the Bureau of Naval Personnel Sea Duty Component when selected for the astronaut program.

During his military service, Herrington logged more than 3,800 flight hours in over thirty different types of aircraft. He was awarded the Navy Commendation Medal, Navy Meritorious Unit Commendation, Coast Guard Meritorious Unit Commendation, Coast Guard Special Operations Service Ribbon, National Defense Service Medal, Sea Service Ribbons (three) and various other service awards.

In 1996, Herrington got a call from NASA. He reported to the Lyndon B. Johnson Space Center, completed two years of training and evaluation and qualified for flight assignment as a mission specialist. Herrington was assigned to the Flight Support Branch of the Astronaut Office, where he served as a member of the Astronaut Support Personnel team responsible for shuttle launch preparations and post-landing operations.

Then, on November 23, 2002, Herrington's dream of space flight became a reality aboard the STS-113 *Endeavour*, the sixteenth shuttle mission to visit the International Space Station. With that mission, he became the first Native American in space.

Mission accomplishments included the delivery of the Expedition-Six crew; the delivery, installation and activation of the P1 Truss; and the transfer of cargo from shuttle to the station. During the mission, Herrington performed three spacewalks, totaling nineteen hours and fifty-five minutes. STS-113 brought home the Expedition-Five crew from their six-month stay aboard the station. The entire mission duration was thirteen days, eighteen hours and forty-seven minutes.

Right: Astronaut John B. Herrington, mission specialist, April 2, 2002. *Courtesy NASA's Shuttle Mission gallery.*

Below: *Front row*: James D. Wetherbee (*right*) and Paul S. Lockhart, commander and pilot, respectively. Attired in training versions of the extravehicular mobility unit (EMU) space suits are astronauts Michael E. Lopez-Alegria (*left*) and John B. Herrington, both mission specialists, November 23, 2002. *NASA's Shuttle Mission gallery.*

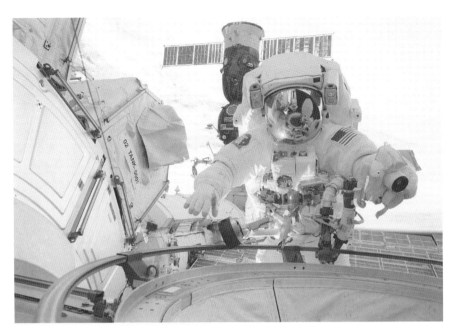

Astronaut Herrington performs his third scheduled spacewalk, November 30, 2002. *NASA's Shuttle Mission gallery.*

As the first enrolled Native American to go into space, Herrington carried a Chickasaw Nation flag, an eagle feather and a native flute, which he played aboard the spaceship. The flag was later presented to the governor of the Chickasaw Nation. Herrington floated the eagle feather inside the shuttle while in space; that feather can now be seen at the Museum of the American Indian at the Smithsonian. "I wanted to honor the tribe, because they supported me and what I was doing," he said.

Herrington's contributions to the space program have even earned him a spot on a coin. The U.S. Mint issued the 2019 Native American one-dollar coin honoring American Indians in the space program. The coin features Herrington as well as Mary Golda Ross of the Cherokee Nation, considered the first Native American engineer in the U.S. space program.[27]

After retiring from NASA in 2005, Herrington has traveled the nation speaking to students, educators, nonprofits and corporations about his unique background in STEM and aviation. He also encourages young Native Americans to work hard and dream big. In 2016, he published a children's book, *Mission to Space*, about his astronaut training at NASA and his mission to the International Space Station. The unique children's book is illustrated with photos from Herrington's training and space travel and includes an English-to-Chickasaw vocabulary list with space-related terms.

"You have to believe in yourself and follow your dreams," he said. "I'm doing something that I never thought I could accomplish."

FROM POVERTY TO COLLEGE FOUNDER

It's always impressive when someone from humble beginnings manages to obtain a college education. But when that person goes on to help start a college, it's even more impressive. That's the incredible story of Fortino Pineda "Tino" Trujillo, one of the founders of Collin College and one of Plano's most beloved and accomplished citizens.

Tino was born on August 12, 1932, in Villa Victoria, Mexico, the eleventh of thirteen children. According to his daughter, Tino's family was "dirt poor" but loved to give back to those who had even less.

Tino attended the University of Mexico City, majoring in economics, and worked as a schoolteacher, federal tax collector, industry inspector and economist for the government of Mexico before immigrating to the United States in 1952. He served in the United States Army and eventually became a partner at his first restaurant in Glendale, California.

After moving to Plano, Texas, he opened Tino's Mexican Restaurant and Cantina in 1976 on Avenue K, where Plano Municipal Center is now located. Plano's population was just forty-three thousand at the time, and those first few years were a struggle.

"It wasn't easy at all when he opened," said Raul Trujillo, Tino's nephew. "There was no business. Tino's shoes had holes in them, so he'd put cardboard in the bottom. But Tino loved making friends and talking to people, and he would not give up."

Eventually, persistence paid off and business picked up. Tino met and married Janie in 1979.

In the early 1980s, Tino's relocated to Collin Creek Mall, and the restaurant quickly became a popular spot in the mall. It was not uncommon for lines to form outside the entrance, and the eatery was busy all day and all evening.

"Tino always greeted us on each visit," said Julie Holmer, a longtime resident. "When it was announced that the restaurant was closing, my family went for our last visit and the place was packed! I ran into so many high school friends who were also there to celebrate this Plano institution."

Music added to the festive feel of the place, and often, Tino would grab the microphone and serenade diners.

"Tino was very social, very good with people," Raul said. "He made a lot of friends, and he remembered their names."

Tino Trujillo at the restaurant. *Courtesy of Raul Trujillo.*

LAUNCHING A COLLEGE

Tino was known for serving the best Mexican food in Plano, but his most lasting accomplishment was helping found Collin County Community College, now Collin College. Tino was integral in the formation and governance of the college district, leading a group of volunteers who obtained signatures to bring the proposal to a vote in April 1985. He was elected to Place 7 on the college's first board of trustees in 1985 and won five elections for six-year terms before retiring in 2014 after nearly thirty years of distinguished service to the college. Family members say Tino was the first person of Hispanic origin elected to public office in Collin County. During his tenure, the college grew from 1,300 students on one campus to nearly 52,000 annually at seven sites.

Colin Chopin, a longtime friend, remembers Tino as an unassuming man who had the respect of many. "He did not put himself forward to become a trustee of the college," he said. "He ran because enough people said, 'C'mon, you need to be on the board.' He had the qualities that led people to want his participation."

In addition to serving on the board of directors for the Collin College Foundation, Tino was involved in the Plano Rotary Club, the Plano Chamber of Commerce, American Cancer Society, Dallas Restaurant Association and Compass Bank of Dallas, as well as service with the Salvation Army of Collin County, Republican Men's Club of Plano, Craig Gilbert Foundation, Hendricks Academy of Honor and Plano Independent School District Advisory Committees for Foreign Language and Career Development. Tino also served on the board of the Plano Conservancy of Historic Preservation—the coauthor of this book!—and established the Taste of Plano food festival. For his contributions to the community, Tino was honored as Plano's Outstanding Citizen of the Year and Small Business Person of the Year, as well as the U.S. Small Business Administration's Minority Small Business Advocate of the Year.

When he passed away at age eighty-two in 2015, the *Dallas Morning News* obituary called Tino "a quiet bridge-builder for numerous civic and business projects in Collin County" and a "kind, gentle and soft-spoken man who united people with needs with others who could help."

Many remembered his love of the community and his patrons.

"Tino truly cared about serving others and was proud to be an American citizen and to serve our country," his obituary said. "He always extended a

Tino (*right*) in front of what was then Collin County Community College when it was under construction. *Courtesy of Collin College.*

helping hand to others, and at his restaurant the most important thing to him was to speak to every single customer that would walk through the door. He wanted you to feel at home while you were there, and would remember your name and your kids' names the next time you came in."

Tino loved to sing at his restaurant and especially enjoyed visiting with his family and friends while trying to get them to eat a pepper that "wasn't hot." He would smile big when he'd succeed with one of his fun pranks. Tino's "restaurant family" was very important to him, and he even had employees who worked for him for more than thirty years.

The current incarnation of Tino's restaurant, Tino's Too, still stands in Plano at the original location on Avenue K. There are still many traces of the beloved Plano icon to be found there. Tino's nephew Raul still works in the restaurant. The tile floor and the decorative tiles on the wall were all installed by Tino himself.

"When we leased this place, it was just a big room," Raul said. "Tino designed everything, and we built the walls with his help."

Raul tries to keep Tino's spirit alive by keeping Tino's Too a friendly local place where visitors can expect a friendly smile and, of course, delicious Mexican food.

THE MIRACLE GAME OF 1977

Every die-hard football fan knows the feeling. Your team has fallen way behind on the scoreboard. Players on the opposing team look like they are gliding along effortlessly, while your boys look like every effort is a slog through the mud. What makes the situation worse is that it's a playoff game; win or go home. This is where the Plano Wildcats and their fans found themselves on December 3, 1977, in old Texas Stadium.

The year 1977 was the inaugural season at John Clark Field (today's John Clark Stadium), named after the legendary coach who led Plano to two state championships in football. Even though the season opened with a 12-point loss to South Garland, hopes were high for another state championship. It would be quite a feat to bookend the opening of the new stadium with a state championship. However, the dream season was turning into a nightmare.

Plano's budding football dynasty had drawn another football power, Highland Park, in the Class 4A State Quarterfinals. Highland Park had dominated opponents all year as they squared off against the 10-1-1 Wildcats.

Early in the third quarter, the Highland Park Scots held a comfortable 28–0 lead. Plano began to mount a comeback. First the defense was able to stop the bleeding and keep the Scots off the scoreboard. The offense came alive and scored two touchdowns to cut the lead to 28–14. Then the defense joined the scoring when Carl Smith intercepted a pitch out and galloped sixty-six yards for a touchdown.

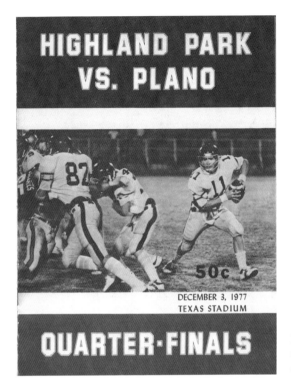

HIGHLAND PARK VS. PLANO

DECEMBER 3, 1977
TEXAS STADIUM

50c

QUARTER-FINALS

Highland Park versus Plano quarterfinals program. *Plano Public Library, Plano, Texas.*

The score now stood at 28–21, with Highland Park clinging to an evaporating lead. The Scots attempted to run out the clock, but Plano got the ball back late in the fourth quarter. As the clock ticked down to thirty-three seconds, Plano executed a flea-flicker with Stevie Haynes completing a pass to Perry Haynes. The play resulted in a sixty-one-yard touchdown, cutting Highland Park's lead to 28–27.

Dismissing the extra point that would tie the game, Plano went for the 2-point conversion. Quarterback Steve Ulmer scampered into the end zone standing up to complete one of the greatest comebacks in Texas high school football history. Final—Plano 29, Highland Park 28. In Plano, the game would become known as the "Miracle Game."

For the state semifinals, Plano traveled to Texas Tech's Jones Stadium in Lubbock. The combination of a great opponent in Odessa Permian and the long trip from Plano to Lubbock made for a long day on the cold Llano Estacado (the plains of northwestern Texas).

Plano would survive that cold day in Lubbock with a punishingly difficult 3–0 victory over the Panthers of Odessa Permian. Plano's defense saved the day with Tim Lassiter intercepting a pass in the end zone, Norris Smith

1965 AA STATE CHAMPS

FRONT ROW: Gary Beard, Tommy Skelton, Danny Minton, Jimmy Merriman, David Peters, Steve Christie, Alan Frazier, Mike Loader, Johnny Pool. MIDDLE ROW: Billy Don Fondren, Jimmy Reed, Mike Johnson, Billy Sangster, James Smithson, Johnny Johnson, Larry Faught, Willie Prince, Gene Berry, Kenneth David. BACK ROW: Rodney Haggard, Donny Herrin, Kenneth Bangs, Neal Olson, Johnny Robinson, Steve Landers, Kent Stout, Hugh Erwin, Ronnie Davies, Carl Grey, Jerry Hayes. NOT SHOWN: John Griggs, Mike Wheeler.

1967 AAA STATE CHAMPS

FRONT ROW: Gary Minton, Lester Havis, Paul Smith, Ronald Cardwell, Johnny Moseley, Richard Randall, Tommy Carroll, Kenneth Newell. MIDDLE ROW: Gene Rushing, David Wood, Weldon Vaughn, Randall Chaddick, James Wilbanks, Darrell Taylor, Alex Williams, John Griggs, Carl McGraw. BACK ROW: Bob Mahler, John Cardwell, David Fondren, Steve George, Mike Wheeler, Albert Hilbun, Donny Peters, Eugene Gaddis, Freddie McIntyre. NOT SHOWN: Vance Maultsby, James Garvey, Gary McCollom, Ray Turner.

1971 AAA STATE CHAMPS

20 Jackie Williams, 21 Chris Spies, 23 Glenn Sanders, 24 Jeff Brumbaugh, 25 Steve Wilson, 26 Doyle Terry, 27 Mike Jones, 28 Pat Thomas, 29 Brad Williams, 30 Bill Standberry, 33 Chip Armstrong, 34 Eugene Majors, 35 Rucker Lewis, 40 Ricky Standberry, 42 Mike Avery, 50 Ross Condit, 52 Paul Tate, 60 Mark Chaddick, 61 Van Nall, 62 Don Standard, 63 Gary Price, 64 Walter Williams, 65 Travis McEntyre, 70 Earl Allen, 71 John Stine, 72 Bill Wray, 73 Zachary Hilbun, 74 Robin Applewhite, 75 Robert Markey, 76 Mike Wood, 77 Bobby Gaddis, 83 David Melson, 81 Grady Dunbar, 82 Ken Bigger, 85 Vic Brooks, 87 Van Davis, 89 Terry Cathey.

1977 AAAA STATE CHAMPS

Trainer Anker Wiggins, Danny Burch, Ray Stone, Carl Smith, Robert Scoggins, Tim Lasiter, Stevie Haynes, Norris Smith, Wes Stover MIDDLE ROWS: Trainer Doug House, Jeff Turner, Brandon King, Rick Stotle, Steve Ulmer, Steve Huber, Perry Haynes, J.P. Shannon, David O'dell, Terry Hill, Joe Neil, Kevin Bush, Mark Burch, Marty Melson, John Gaddis, Tim Braden, Mike Pedigo, Bill Tabor, Mike Sartain, Shawn Stanton, Tony Dent. BACK ROW: Steve Perryman, John Muns, Kenneth Wilson, C.M. Pier, Kevin Jennings, Brian Jones, Billy Ray Smith, Mike Witte, Larry Albertson, Dee Herrin.

The Plano Wildcats' four winning teams from 1965, 1967, 1971 and 1977. Note that the school moved up from AA to AAAA in those twelve years. *Plano Public Library, Plano, Texas.*

1977 Wildcats—State Champions. *Plano Public Library, Plano, Texas.*

blocking a fifty-two-yard field goal attempt and Carl Smith blocking a twenty-seven-yard field goal attempt.

The next week, the largest crowd to ever attend a Texas high school playoff game (49,953) arrived to see the Wildcats take on Port Neches-Groves for the 4A State Championship. Back in the friendly confines of Texas Stadium, Plano defeated Port Neches-Groves 13–10 to win its fourth state championship—a championship that would have never happened without the miracle game of 1977.

Postscript: Just as Hidden History *was nearing completion, quarterback Steve Ulmer passed away on April 5, 2019, at the age of fifty-eight. Though not possessing the size, speed or arm strength of other blue-chip quarterbacks, Ulmer's heart, grit and strong work ethic all ensure that he will be remembered as a champion.*

COLLIN CREEK'S MALL TUNNELS

Hidden under the massive parking lot of Collin Creek Mall are some spooky passageways unknown to many Plano residents: a series of tunnels that allow Spring Creek to flow under the shopping center. When developers built the mall back in the early 1980s, one of their biggest challenges was how to accommodate Spring Creek, which ran through the property. They decided to build three culverts (concrete tunnels), each of them almost a half mile long. The creek's waters flow over concrete, through the culverts, from 15th Street to Plano Parkway. (You can spot the north end of the culverts behind the Big Lots store currently located on 15th Street.)

In the 1980s, rumor had it that the tunnels were "haunted" and a lure for local Satanists. Certainly, they're dark and creepy enough to get the imagination going.

When you enter a tunnel, you can see light at the other end—but it's deceptive. The farther you proceed, the darker the tunnel becomes, until you get close to the other end. Deep inside the structure, adventurous urban spelunkers have encountered a "room" that connects the three culverts.

One of those urban explorers, Eric Kuhns, was brave enough to explore the room. "You see what looks like bloody handprints and satanic symbols," he said. "There's an inscription in one spot that says, 'He is watching you.' It's pretty creepy."

Even though they were technically off-limits to the public, the tunnels were a popular hangout for teens during the mall's heyday. Some longtime residents remember riding their bikes down in the tunnels. One reports

Inside the tunnels underneath Collin Creek Mall. *Photos by Eric Kuhns/Koonagi Media.*

"getting lucky" there a few times, whereas another says, "I'm glad those tunnels can't talk."

Hava Johnston, founder of a Facebook group with more than eight thousand members called "Collin Creek Mall: An Era Gone By," remembers the tunnels well. "As kids we drank beer and told spooky stories in the tunnels, and no, we shouldn't have, but it was all in fun and most of us all turned out all right," she said.

City crews converge inside the dark culverts several times a year to remove accumulated silt and debris and to clear a path for the water, as well as for periodic inspections of the structure. Like the mall, the culverts are aging, so the inspections are especially important. In the past, crews have installed metal ribs to reinforce the ceiling in the walls where they were starting to cave in.

Centurion American Development Group recently purchased Collin Creek Mall and launched ambitious plans to demolish part of the mall and rebuild it with shops, restaurants and a variety of homes at the location. However, it's too early to know what will happen to one of Plano's best kept secrets: the "haunted" tunnels of Collin Creek Mall.

The Cockroach Hall of Fame Museum

U ntil 2012, Plano was home to a unique attraction: the Cockroach Hall of Fame Museum.

"It is not the Smithsonian," as owner Michael Bohdan liked to say—but it was an interesting enough oddity to merit an appearance on the *Tonight Show* and mentions on websites like Atlas Obscura and Roadside America.

You had to know where to look for it. The museum was part of the Pest Shop, a small do-it-yourself shop that sold extermination products for getting rid of pests in your home—ants, mice, roaches, rats and more. The shop is still located at the corner of Custer and 15th.

Visitors were treated to exhibits like the Bates Roach Motel office, which featured a roach dressed in a housecoat and wig that moved along a track from the office to Room 1 with a tiny knife in its hand, and a collection of "celebrity" roaches with names like Elvis, David Letterroach and Liberoachi.

Bohdan, sporting a roach-bedecked hat, guided visitors through the museum. And he knew what he was talking about—Bohdan earned a bachelor's degree in zoology from Southern Illinois University at Carbondale.

As one reviewer wrote on Roadside America about Bohdan, "He'll stop mid-convo (talking about his old 'Last Supper with roaches' diorama) and help customers with problems with skunks, then hop right back into his old stories about his nationwide competitions for roach art." Another remembers Bohdan handing out free samples of barbecue-flavored larvae.

Visitors Aiden and Ivy Shertzer with owner Michael Bohdan at the Cockroach Hall of Fame Museum. *Courtesy Jennifer Shertzer,* Plano Magazine.

The cockroach museum was definitely a hidden treasure, one that many Plano residents didn't know about. One resident, John Brooks, remembers first seeing Bohdan on the *Tonight Show* with Johnny Carson. Another lifelong resident, Ryan Dry, recalls first learning about the museum by way of an article about "oddities of the world," with a mention of Plano's cockroach museum. "I was shocked to learn it was half a block from my house!" he said.

The Pest Shop is still open, under new management, but alas, the Cockroach Hall of Fame Museum is no more. Michael Bohdan retired to Phoenix and later returned to Dallas. He still has his cockroach displays and hopes that one day he can find the right place to resurrect the Cockroach Hall of Fame Museum.

DOWNTOWN PLANO MURALS

In January 2017, the Plano Art Association and the Historic Downtown Plano Association partnered to launch the Downtown Mural Project to bring the first set of murals to the Downtown Plano Arts District. Made possible by a grant from the Plano Heritage Commission, the project uses visual art to celebrate Plano's rich history and the area's recent designation as the Downtown Plano Arts District by the Texas Commission for the Arts.

To assist in the artists' open call and overall project management of the mural installations, Plano Art Association enlisted the help of Joshua King, a Dallas-based artist. An advisory council was also formed to ensure the historical accuracy and relevance of the murals.

The first of the three murals was completed in July 2017 and is located on the west-facing wall of Georgia's Farmers' Market. It was painted by local DFW artist Will Heron and incorporates historical elements inspired by Plano's past. Each of the mural's five columns is a different color and focuses on elements taken from historic photos of Plano, submitted by residents earlier that year.

Artist Wes Hardin painted the second mural, located at Vickery Park by the DART station, in September 2017. The mural displays a scene from historic Plano, with citizens strolling through a downtown bustling with merchants and commuter passengers. The famous Texas Electric Railway interurban railcar is featured, as well as the storefronts of downtown Plano buildings. The whole scene is set in front of a colorful Texas sunset.

Mural in downtown Plano, completed in 2017 by artist Will Heron. *Photo by Jeff Campbell.*

Located near the DART Rail station, this mural in downtown Plano was completed in 2017 by Wes Hardin. *Photo by Jeff Campbell.*

This three-dimensional mural was installed in 2017 at the corner of Avenue K and 15th. Called *ECHOWAVE: Listen to the Echoes of Plano's History*, the piece features audio segments about Plano's history. *Photo by Jeff Campbell.*

The third and final downtown Plano mural was installed in December 2017. The piece is a three-dimensional mural, located on the southwest corner of Avenue K and 15th Street in the arts district. The mural has both visual and audio components, featuring four metal representations of sound waves between the letters P-L-A-N-O.

Each sound wave has a corresponding recorded audio segment depicting a different historical event from Plano's past. A plaque in front of the mural reads "ECHOWAVE: Listen to the Echoes of Plano's History." The four audio segments tell listeners about Plano's name and origins; the founding of the fire department; business and commerce; and Plano's railroad heritage. The audio segments are narrated by Mayor Harry LaRosiliere, Plano fire chief Sam Greif, executive director of the Plano Chamber of Commerce Jamee Jolly and Robert Haynes, curator of the Interurban Railway Museum.[28]

BUTCHERS' LAST STAND

Some folks can personally remember a local butcher shop. Some have just seen one on TV. The old-fashioned local butcher shop was a place with a neighborly feel, where the customer and owner knew each other on a first name basis, a place to get advice on the best way to prepare a special meal or to order a cut of meat just the way you liked it. Fortunately, these shops have not all been relegated to the past. In fact, you can find one such shop at Hirsch's Meat Market.

Many Planoites frequent Hirsch's Meat Market, so it's hardly a secret. But what you may not know is that Hirsch's provides a kind of specialty service that is quickly disappearing. Hirsch's Meat Market opened in Plano in 1992 and has been at its present location, 1301 West Parker Road, for fourteen years.

Before opening his own market, Gary Hirsch worked as a butcher in a chain grocery store. There, he began to see changes in the industry that, in his mind, were not for the better. According to Gary, chain grocery stores began selling a lower grade of meat that was already prepackaged to keep prices low. The craft of the butcher was now reduced to the role of a simple meat cutter. As he explained, a butcher takes an entire side of beef and breaks it down to primal cuts, while a meat cutter simply prepares those cuts for sale. It's like the difference between a chef and a line cook. Hirsch's Meat Market requires a two-year apprenticeship to become a full-fledged butcher in the shop.

Right: Gary Hirsch of Hirsch's Meats. *Photo by Jennifer Shertzer, courtesy of* Plano Magazine.

Below: Inside Hirsch's Meats. *Photo by Jennifer Shertzer, courtesy of* Plano Magazine.

Hirsch's employs between sixteen and twenty staff members, including a chef to advise customers on the best way to prepare their purchase or the best side items and wine to serve with the meal. Gary's knowledgeable staff keeps Hirsch's a cut above on customer service, something Gary feels the industry has lost over the years.

Gary buys meat from all over the country, seeking out the best quality he can find. Besides beef, the butcher shop also carries pork, chicken and sausage. His team produces thirty-six different sausages in house and also makes its own signature crab dip. Hirsch's also sells twenty varieties of wood for smoking meats at home.

When asked, "What is the best steak that someone could purchase from Hirsch's to prepare at home?" Gary suggested two: a wagyu and a dry-aged rib-eye.

Wagyu is a Japanese breed of cow; the word literally translates into *wa*, meaning Japanese, and *gyu*, meaning cow. Wagyu is prized for its fat marbling. Wagyu cattle genetically have more omega-3 and omega-6 fatty acids than other breeds of cattle. This produces an extremely tender steak with a buttery flavor that melts in your mouth. In 1975, wagyu cattle began to be imported to the United States. Now in the country there are pure-bred wagyu and also wagyu cattle that are cross-bred with Black Angus cattle to produce the American-style Kobe beef crossbreed.

A dry-aged rib-eye is produced by hanging the meat in a refrigerated unit at thirty-four degrees for about a month. The dry-aging process allows moisture to evaporate from the meat, creating a greater concentration of flavors. Enzymes in the meat are also broken down, which makes the meat more tender. The process is time consuming and reduces the weight of the meat—two reasons you will not find a dry-aged rib-eye in your local big-box grocery store.

Another perk of shopping at a specialty butcher shop is the high level of client care. Gary is very proud of the relationships he has built over the years. Today, he serves the grown sons and daughters of some of his original shoppers. Even long-term customers who have moved to other parts of the country come back once or twice a year to stock up at Hirsch's Meat Market.

Visit Hirsch's today to experience customer service of the past and see why loyalty is always in stock at this long-lasting butcher shop.

This story originally appeared in Plano Magazine, *February 11, 2019.*

FAMOUS PEOPLE FROM PLANO

The city of Plano has been honored with a laundry list of awards and distinctions, ranging from Best Place to Live If You Want to Get Rich (Thrillist, 2019) to Second Most Educated City in the U.S. (*Men's Health* magazine, 2011). So it's not surprising that many accomplished and well-known people either hail from Plano or call Plano home today. Here's a far-from-exhaustive list of just a few of Plano's most famous folks.

SCIENCE

Anousheh Ansari. *Wikimedia Commons.*

On September 18, 2006, a few days after her fortieth birthday, Plano resident **Anousheh Ansari** became the first Iranian in space, the fourth overall self-funded space tourist and the first self-funded woman to fly to the International Space Station. Ansari is an Iranian American engineer and co-founder and chairwoman of Prodea Systems. Her previous business accomplishments include serving as co-founder and CEO of Telecom Technologies, Inc. (TTI). Her memoir, *My Dream of Stars*, co-written with Homer Hickam, was published by Palgrave Macmillan in 2010.

ACTORS AND ENTERTAINERS

Alan Wray Tudyk. *Wikimedia Commons.*

Who's the person from Plano most frequently looked up on Wikipedia? That distinction goes to **Alan Wray Tudyk**, an American actor and voice actor known for his roles as Hoban "Wash" Washburne in the space western series *Firefly* and the film *Serenity*. He has also had starring roles in the films *DodgeBall: A True Underdog Story*; *I, Robot*; *A Knight's Tale*; *42*; *Maze Runner: The Scorch Trials*; *and Rogue One*. He has voiced characters in every Walt Disney Animation Studios feature film since *Wreck-It Ralph* in 2012, including Iago in the 2019 live-action adaptation of *Aladdin*. He wrote, directed and starred in the comedy web series *Con Man* (2015–17) about a struggling actor whose career is still defined by a successful science fiction TV show he was once on, loosely based on Tudyk's own experience having been on *Firefly*. The series aired on Syfy in 2017 and earned him a Primetime Emmy Award nomination.

Perhaps Plano's most famous Eagle Scout is **Travis Tope**, an actor who played Charlie Miller in the 2016 science-fiction disaster film *Independence Day: Resurgence* and Joe Harper in the series *Boardwalk Empire*. In January 2010, as a member of Plano's Boy Scout Troop 1000, Tope was awarded the rank of Eagle Scout.

Other Plano-based, Plano-born or Plano-raised stars include **Chace Crawford**, the actor who portrayed Nate Archibald on The CW's teen drama series *Gossip Girl* (2007–12); **Kevin McHale**, an actor, singer, dancer and radio personality best known for his role in the Fox comedy-drama series *Glee*; **Boz Scaggs**, singer, songwriter and guitarist whose albums topped the charts in the late 1970s; **Meenakshi Seshadri**, a Bollywood actress who mainly appeared in Hindi, Tamil and Telugu films and moved to Plano after concluding her film career to raise her children and run a dance school; **Thomas Joseph "T.J." Thyne**, best known for his role in the TV series *Bones* as Dr. Jack Hodgins, an entomologist, mineralogist and botanist; and **Michael Urie**, a TV and Broadway actor best known for his role as Marc St. James in the TV series *Ugly Betty*.

SPORTS

Rex Burkhead is a Plano Senior High graduate, a running back for the New England Patriots and a Super Bowl Champion. He played college football at Nebraska and was drafted by the Cincinnati Bengals in the sixth round of the 2013 NFL Draft. Burkhead keeps a home in Plano and hosts an annual fundraiser in Plano for Team Jack, a charity that raises money for pediatric brain cancer research. At Super Bowl LIII in 2019, Burkhead wasn't the only Planoite in the game. **Joseph Noteboom**, also a Plano Senior grad, was also there—a rookie for the opposing team, the Los Angeles Rams.

Rex Burkhead. *Wikimedia Commons.*

Jake Arrieta is a Cy Young Award–winning pitcher for 2016 World Series champion Chicago Cubs, a Plano East alumnus and now a pitcher for the Philadelphia Phillies. He previously played for the Baltimore Orioles. As a high school senior, he was selected by the Cincinnati Reds in the thirty-first round of the 2004 draft, but instead he chose to attend college. Arrieta played college baseball at Weatherford Junior College and at Texas Christian University (TCU). He made his big-league debut for the Orioles in 2010, and after four seasons, Arrieta was traded to the Cubs in 2013. In 2015, he led MLB in wins with twenty-two, pitched a no-hitter and won the 2015 National League Cy Young Award. In 2016, Arrieta was an NL All-Star, threw his second no-hitter, was awarded a Silver Slugger Award and won a World Series with the Cubs. Prior to the start

Jake Arrieta. *Wikimedia Commons.*

of the 2018 season, Arrieta signed a three-year, $75 million contract as a free agent with the Phillies.

History Uncovered

Officer Rye's death merited just a short mention in a Plano history book published in the 1950s. In the early 2000s, that blurb caught the eye of Detective Luke Grant, a Plano police officer since 1983. He was intrigued.

Officer Grant, a history and genealogy buff, decided to do a little detective work to learn more. He visited libraries in Plano, McKinney, Dallas and Durant, Oklahoma, and combed through history books and microfilms of old newspapers.

He learned that Rye, fifty-two, had served with the Plano Police Department for eighteen months when he was felled by a .45-caliber bullet from a handgun. To his surprise, one newspaper article described Officer Rye as a sworn officer with a badge, a gun and full arrest powers.

That was an important discovery.

"Because most accounts referred to Rye as a night watchman, everyone had assumed that he was a security guard," said Officer Grant. But as a sworn officer, Rye was a "brother in blue"—an officer who had died in the line of duty, someone whose memory would be honored by fellow officers, in Plano and beyond.

Soon, Officer Grant had solved one mystery: Why had Officer Rye's death been so quickly overlooked in Plano?

First, Rye was one of just two men who composed law enforcement in Plano, which was a small town in 1920. The other man left the force within a year. Also, Rye's widow and children left Plano immediately after his death. He was buried in San Saba, Texas, and the family stayed there, never returning to Plano. His funeral notice in the local newspaper noted he was a member of San Saba's Baptist church, "a good man and citizen… who lived and labored in San Saba for a number of years and had many friends here."

Finding the Family

But Officer Grant needed more proof than a newspaper clipping to have Officer Rye's name added to state and national memorials for fallen officers. He tracked down Rye's granddaughter Molly Lane in Austin. When they connected by telephone, she became emotional. She told Officer Grant that she'd inherited her grandfather's tin badge.

Above: Officer Rye and his family. *Courtesy Plano Police Department.*

Right: Officer Rye's badge and pistol. *Courtesy Plano Police Department.*

Officer Grant held his breath as he asked her to read the inscription on the badge.

"Police, Plano, Texas," Molly said. That was the missing piece of evidence needed to prove that Rye was a lawman.

Molly shared how her grandfather's death had traumatized the family and how she had attempted to get the state to acknowledge her grandfather's sacrifice, with no luck. Her mother, who was ten when her father was killed, relived that fateful morning from time to time until her death at age ninety-one in 2000. As Molly told the *Dallas Morning News*, "Every time a police officer got killed, she'd come to me and say, 'They've killed my daddy. They've killed my daddy.'…It just messed with her head."

Officer Grant and Police Chief Greg Rushin traveled to Austin to visit the family and pay their respects. Molly graciously donated the badge, and another family member donated Rye's pistol. They shared family photos, which Officer Grant added to the stuffed, three-inch notebook in which he carefully filed the records and notes related to the case.

Molly also gave him a copy of Rye's funeral notice in the San Saba newspaper, which closed with these poignant words: "Whether he was shot from ambush and then discharged his own pistol to alarm the people and call for help, or whether he was engaged in an effort to stop the bold robbers will likely remain a mystery as he was unable to tell the story after assistance came to him. But in either case, Green Wesley Rye died like a brave man doing his duty."

COLD CASE

When he started his research, Officer Grant initially began looking through newspapers in 1921 because of an error—he'd simply written down the wrong year in his notes. He calls that mistake a "God moment"—a bit of divine intervention that helped him uncover more information, previously forgotten, about who killed Officer Rye.

Newspaper articles in March 1921 said that Dallas's chief of detectives and the Collin County sheriff had traveled to a city jail in Durant, Oklahoma, to question a man who confessed to taking part in a bank robbery in Plano.

Now Officer Grant was presented with a tantalizing possibility. Could he solve the cold case of who murdered Green Wesley Rye more than eighty years earlier?

Officer Grant traveled to Durant to pore through prison records and files of the Durant newspaper. He learned that the man, Alfred Gonia, was a career criminal who confessed he was one of four men and a woman who had robbed the Plano National Bank. Gonia claimed he was just the lookout—he hadn't killed anyone, just fired a few warning shots. He had collected $1,300 (equivalent to about $16,000 in 2018) from the heist.

But during a break from questioning, Gonia attempted to kill himself, using a sharpened spoon to cut his own throat. After that, he would never discuss the burglary again. Officer Grant traced Gonia's prison career until 1934, when he was released from the Kansas Penitentiary. And then the trail goes cold.

We'll probably never get a definitive answer about who killed Green Wesley Rye, Officer Grant said, but "I believe in my heart that Gonia is the shooter."

Alfred Gonia, the man whom Luke Grant believes killed Green Wesley Rye. *Courtesy Plano Police Department.*

SURPRISE WITNESS

There was one more surprise in store for Officer Grant.

On February 27, 2003, almost exactly eighty-three years after Rye's death, the *Dallas Morning News* ran a story about Officer Grant's detective work and Officer Rye's sacrifice, with the headline "The Lawman that History Forgot." The article concluded with a plea from Officer Grant for anyone with information about the case to call, with a telephone number.

Someone did call. Officer Grant received a phone call from an elderly woman named Anna May Shaw.

"I guess you didn't figure you'd hear from an eyewitness," she said.

Anna May, age eighty-eight, was the daughter of J.J. Vavra, the baker, and was just four years old when Rye was killed.

She recalled how her mother had heard the shots and, fearing her husband had been robbed, grabbed a pistol. Her mother saw two men running across the railroad tracks and shot at them but missed.

Anna May Shaw also remembered vividly how Rye's body was carried into the bedroom in her parents' house. His eyes were still open, but he didn't move, which had confused her.

"I can't remember what I ate for breakfast today, but I can still remember that scene as if it happened yesterday," she told Grant.

IN THE LINE OF DUTY

Rye remained the only Plano officer lost in the line of duty until July 7, 2007, when Officer Dayle Weston "Wes" Hardy was killed in a traffic accident. Now, every year, Plano police hold a ceremony honoring the city's two fallen officers: Traffic Officer Wes Hardy and Deputy City Marshal Green Wesley Rye—one of recent memory, and the other almost one hundred years ago, whose story was almost lost to us.

Today, Green Wesley Rye is far from forgotten. Thanks to Detective Grant's research, a plaque commemorating his sacrifice was installed across the street from the A.R. Schell Building on 15th Street—the same building that once housed the Plano National Bank. Some of Rye's descendants traveled to Plano for the installation.

Every February 28, the Plano police dispatcher announces an "End of Watch," and members of the force pause to remember Officer Rye. Each class of new Plano Police Department recruits completes the Green Wesley Rye Memorial Run, a two-mile trek that takes the soon-to-be officers past the spot where Rye was shot.

If you visit the Plano Police Department's headquarters, you'll see a portrait on the wall honoring Rye—the first Plano law enforcement officer to die in the line of duty. Rye's name is inscribed in the memorial in Austin.

There's also a page honoring Rye on a national website, the "Officer Down Memorial Page: Remembering All of Law Enforcement's Heroes." There, visitors can post words of reflections. The comments on Officer Rye's page serve as poignant reminders of the kinship that police officers share with their brothers and sisters in blue—even one lost almost one hundred years ago.

"Your watch has ended but the memory of your service remains. Rest in Peace my brother," wrote a Plano police officer.

Another officer offered this poem, author unknown, imagining a police officer standing before God on judgment day:

A monument across from the Schell Building, where Rye was shot, commemorates his sacrifice. *Photo by Mary Jacobs.*

Step forward now, Officer. You've borne your burdens well.
Come walk a beat on heaven's streets.
You've done your time in hell

Plano salutes you, Officer Hardy and Officer Rye. May your sacrifices never be forgotten.

NOTES

A Brief History of Plano

1. *Cruising Historical Collin County*, brochure published by the Collin County Historical Commission.
2. Friends of the Plano Public Library, *Plano: The Early Years* (Wolfe City, TX: Henington Publishing Company, 1996), 5.
3. *Cruising Historical Collin County*.

Plano's Oldest Tree

4. Evelyn Harding, "Honoring Plano's Bicentennial Tree," www.plano.gov/DocumentCenter/View/329/Bicentennial-Tree-History?bidId=.

Henry Cook

5. Friends of the Plano Public Library, *Plano: The Early Years*, 71, citing the October 1888 edition of *Plano Review*, which said, "In the year 1845 Collin County was a wild waste."
6. *Plano: The Early Years* says "Kaskaski," but that is likely a misspelling. Kaskaskia, Illinois, has its own interesting history; two of the officers whom Cook served under also hailed from Kaskaskia. See Illinois War

of 1812 Society, illinois1812warsociety.org/gallery.html, and Wikipedia, "Kaskaskia, Illinois," en.wikipedia.org/wiki/Kaskaskia,_Illinois.

7. Friends of the Plano Public Library, *Plano: The Early Years*, 71.

8. Henry's wives were Elizabeth McCormick (or possibly McCormack), whom he married in 1800; Nellie Waddle, married 1805; Alcy or Elsie Nix, married 1811; and Sarah "Sally" Kincaid (1793–1889), married 1825.

9. Henry Cook came to Texas on the heels of two of his grown children from an earlier marriage—David Cook and Mary Ann Cook Miller—who had settled in North Texas in 1845, along with a party of six others. They settled in Trinity Mill, a now-extinct community near where Trinity Mills Road is now located in Carrollton. The next year, Henry followed, leaving Illinois in a caravan of seven wagons. Three wagons carried Henry; his wife, Sarah; and six children. Four additional wagons carried John Nix, John McCann, Josh McCann (a married son of John McCann) and Bill Miller, whose wife was a twin sister of Josh McCann. Two pigs and a few chickens tagged along.

10. Bullock Museum, "Frontier Folk: Texas Has Always Been the Place to Be," www.thestoryoftexas.com/discover/campfire-stories/frontier-folk.

11. Timelines of History, "Timeline Texas," www.timelines.ws/states/TEXAS.HTML.

12. Bullock Museum, "Frontier Folk."

13. Friends of the Plano Public Library, *Plano: The Early Years*, 69.

14. Ibid., 141.

15. Jennifer Grimm, "Willow Bend Church Celebrates 160 Years," *Plano Star Courier*, February 12, 2010, starlocalmedia.com/newsflagcontributed/willow-bend-church-celebrates-years/article_20bbc9b2-68d7-551d-8b26-92e01c701964.html.

16. As cited in Friends of the Plano Public Library, *Plano: The Early Years*; J. Lee Stambaugh and Lillian J. Stambaugh, *History of Collin County* (Austin: Texas State Historical Association, 1958), 28.

Mule Captial of the World

17. Friends of the Plano Public Library, *Plano: The Early Years*, 41.

Death Is a Salesman

18. Donald R. Hopkins, MD, MPH, "Smallpox: Ten Years Gone," *American Journal of Public Health* (December 1988).
19. "The Child Whose Town Rejected Vaccines," Wellcome Collection, July 13, 2017, wellcomecollection.org.

Plano's Fire Bell

20. *Plano Fire and Rescue: 125 Years of Serving, 1886–2011* (Evansville, IN: M.T. Publishing Company, Inc., 2012).

Pagoda on the Prairie

21. John Merwin, "The Strange Case of Plano University," *D Magazine*, January 1975, www.dmagazine.com/publications/d-magazine/1975/january/the-strange-case-of-plano-university.
22. Joshua Baethge, "Gone and Mostly Forgotten: Short-Lived University of Plano Dedicated 50 Years Ago," *Plano Star Courier*, April 1, 2016.
23. Committee on Children with Disabilities, American Academy of Pediatrics, P.R. Ziring, D. Brazdziunas, W.C. Cooley, et al., "The Treatment of Neurologically Impaired Children Using Patterning." *Pediatrics* 104 (1999): 1149–51. doi:10.1542/peds.104.5.1149. PMID 10545565.

A Native American in Space

24. Chickasaw TV, "John Herrington: Chickasaw Determination," 2014, www.chickasaw.tv/videos/john-herrington-profiles-of-a-nation; Chickasaw TV, "John Herrington," 2017, www.chickasaw.tv/episodes/profiles-of-a-nation-season-1-episode-1-john-herrington.
25. Rebecca Wallick, "John Herrington: College Dropout Becomes NASA Astronaut and Walks in Space," *McCall Digest*, 2018, mccalldigest.com/john-herrington-college-dropout-becomes-nasa-astronaut-and-walks-in-space.
26. NASA, "Biographical Data: John Bennett Herrington," www.nasa.gov/sites/default/files/atoms/files/herrington_john.pdf.

27. United States Mint, "2019 Native American $1 Coin," www.usmint.gov/coins/coin-medal-programs/native-american-dollar-coins/2019-american-indians-in-space.

Downtown Plano Murals

28. Historic Downtown Plano, "The Downtown Mural Project," www.visitdowntownplano.com/the-downtown-mural-project.

About the Authors

MARY JACOBS is the producer of *Plano Podcast* and a freelance writer who writes regularly for the *Dallas Morning News*, the *Silver Century* and other outlets. Mary was one of the founding organizers of TEDxPlano in 2014 and served as a speaker in 2017. In 2018, The History Press published Mary's first book, *Haunted Plano, Texas*.

JEFF CAMPBELL is executive director of the Plano Conservancy for Historic Preservation. He writes about Plano history for *Plano Magazine* and also coauthored *Football and Integration in Plano, Texas: Stay in There, Wildcats!* (The History Press, 2014) and *Plano's Historic Cemeteries* (Arcadia Publishing, 2014). Jeff has worked on historic preservation projects in Texas, Louisiana and New Mexico. He serves on the board of the Texas chapter of the Association of Gravestone Studies and on the advisory board of Texas Dance Hall Preservation and is a chapter representative for the Forest Fire Lookout Association.

Cheryl Smith is a public services librarian with the Plano Public Library. Through her library work as a genealogy research expert, she has helped make Collin County historic images and documents available for public viewing online and has transcribed many of the handwritten documents, diaries and notes in the Plano Public Library collections, including those of the Plano Volunteer Fire Department and the Thursday Study Club.